T0243972

**Bagna Cauda
Crudité**
(Five of Coins)

**Black Sesame Butter
Parker House Rolls**
(Death)

Death

**Lavender
Celebration Spritz**
(The Tower)

DIVINE
YOUR
DINNER

A COOKBOOK FOR USING TAROT AS
YOUR GUIDE TO MAGICKAL MEALS

Courtney McBroom & Melinda Lee Holm

Clarkson Potter/Publishers
New York

Over the past decade, our society has become much more aware of the quality and sustainability of food and the importance of a diet that fits our individual health needs. In an eating revolution that's already anchored in mindfulness, *Divine Your Dinner* is the next step toward integrating purpose into your palate.

The seed of this book was planted during a happy hour date at one of our favorite local watering holes (RIP Malo). Over some crispy ground beef tacos (which we re-created on page 70) and spicy margaritas, we got to talking about which is better: a spicy margarita or a regular one. Courtney argued that the simplicity of the standard margarita allows the flavor and integrity of the spirit to shine through. Melinda countered that spicy is better because chiles make us feel energetic, creative, and magickal through their transmission of Elemental Fire energy. And thus, the Great Culinary Magick Debates began!

That day, our favorite game emerged. Anytime we hung out and food was involved, we bounced around recipe ideas based on ingredients used in magick spells and rituals. We got really good at crafting menus around the energies we wanted to invite into our lives and bodies. With Melinda's magickal prowess and Courtney's food expertise, we matched food energies with tarot cards and, well, it was magick! The Sun flooded the light of clarity down upon us, the Ace of Swords spoke the truth of the ages, and the Emperor demanded it: We *had* to make a full deck of tarot recipes.

Even if you know nothing about tarot or why we spell "magick" with that "k" at the end, you can start integrating this sacred wisdom into your cooking right now. In fact, as you explore the recipes in these pages, you just might discover that you've been a kitchen witch all along! Here's the thing—we didn't invent magickal cooking. Throughout history, humans have been using common ingredients for uncommon purposes. Call it a folk remedy, call it a spell, call it being a hippie—kitchen witches know that food affects a lot more than just your stomach. Scratch the surface of any spell book and you'll find all sorts of familiar faces from your pantry. Bay leaf, thyme, even salt. (*Especially* salt!) We've matched common ingredients up with the energies of tarot cards, allowing you to experience their power with maximum deliciousness.

Still fuzzy on how all this works? Not to worry. Read on for a quick tutorial on tarot (Tarot 101, page 8), an explanation of what on Earth we were thinking (Divine Inspiration, page 10), and how you can join our little coven and start divining your dinner (Ways to Use This Book, page 11). There's also a handy list of our magickal ingredients and their properties (Magickal Ingredient Pantry, page 12).

MAGICK VS MAGIC ★ ADDING A "K" TO "MAGIC" IS A CONVENTION USED TO DIFFERENTIATE PRACTICES INTENDED TO MAKE A REAL IMPACT ON ONE'S LIFE FROM SHOW MAGIC (RABBITS OUT OF HATS AND THAT SORT OF THING).

TAROT
101

Before we get into the nitty-gritty of how this book can connect you with your innate magickal self (making you the most sought-after potluck guest in town), let's take a moment to make sure we're all on the same page with what tarot is, why it's so rad to use it in cooking, and our strategy for creating the best possible recipe for each card. But first things first . . .

YE OLDEN THYMES

Tarot decks have been around since at least the mid-fifteenth century when wealthy families in southern Europe had fancy decks of cards hand-painted for fun and status. While these decks were originally made for card games, we now know them as a tool for divination—for gaining insight into situations through magickal means.

Tarot decks are made up of seventy-eight cards, fifty-six of which are organized by suits, similar to modern playing card decks. These suited cards are collectively referred to as the Minor Arcana. The other twenty-two cards have no suit, but they do have formal names and numbers. These cards are called the Major Arcana. All tarot decks conform to this structure.

THERE ARE MANY KINDS OF DECKS USED FOR DIVINATION. LENORMAND DECKS HAVE THEIR OWN SPECIFIC STRUCTURE AND THERE ARE MANY OTHERS THAT DO NOT FOLLOW ANY PARTICULAR STRUCTURE—THESE ARE CALLED ORACLE DECKS.

TAROT TODAY

There is a growing movement of readers and mystics using tarot and divination for spiritual growth, personal empowerment, and even therapy! Instead of predicting a set outcome, these readers open up possibilities by unveiling larger truths, hidden gems, and pitfalls in the cosmic field. This is Melinda's position on tarot and the one we take in this book. With this view in mind, here's a little breakdown of the cards and the roles they play.

The Major Arcana
The majors are, well, major. These cards represent *big* energies. The kind you maybe take a whole lifetime to move through or master. These cards tend to describe who we are and who we are invited to become. You may recognize some of the characters here—The Magician, Death, The Moon—from their appearances in the folk tales of southern Europe that inspired these cards and from myths and legends all over the world. Archetypes are like that. They tend to really get around.

The Minor Arcana
The Minor Arcana cards are divided into four suits—Swords, Wands, Cups, and Coins—each of which corresponds to one of the four classical elements—Air, Fire, Water, and Earth, respectively. Each suit has ten numbered cards (Ace through Ten) and four court cards (Page, Knight, Queen, King). The names of the court cards may vary between decks, but there are always four. Each court figure also gets their own elemental association, teaching us the subtle ways each element can manifest.

WHENEVER YOU SEE A FAMILIAR NOUN CAPITALIZED, YOU'LL KNOW IT IS REFERRING TO THE ALCHEMICAL ELEMENT AND NOT THE STANDARD NOUN. FOR EXAMPLE, "Fire" REFERS TO THE MAGICKAL ELEMENT THAT INSPIRES ACTION AND INTUITION, WHILE "fire" REFERS TO THAT THING THAT BURNS YOU.

The tarot interpretations provided for you to *Divine Your Dinner* are rooted in tradition, yet are updated to be relevant to modern life. As Melinda does in her readings, we invite you to view all the cards and archetypes as available and integral to everyone—all gender identities and expressions, all ages, all ethnicities, all abilities. We feel confident that as you make your way through these recipes, you will recognize a part of yourself in each of the cards.

DIVINE INSPIRATION

Now that you're a newly minted tarot expert, we'll let you in on the secrets of our kitchen magick. We've assigned recipes to cards in two different ways.

For the **Major Arcana**, Melinda started by choosing ingredients emblematic of the wisdom of each card (and that she uses in rituals and spell-work). Courtney created recipes around each ingredient to invoke the magick of the ingredients and make them a delight to integrate into your physical being (i.e., eat them).

The **Minor Arcana** recipes are divided into culinary categories to match the element associated with each suit:

SUIT	ELEMENT	PLATE
SWORDS	AIR	POULTRY
WANDS	FIRE	MEATS
CUPS	WATER	SEAFOOD
COINS	EARTH	VEGGIES & GRAINS

The court cards are where we let our hair down a little. We wanted to add desserts to the mix and this seemed a great place to do it. Since the court card roles also carry an elemental energy (Earth for Pages, Fire for Knights, Water for Queens, Air for Kings), you'll find a little of their vibe in each recipe, intermingling with the vibe of the suit in subtle and not so subtle ways (hello, flambés!).

We hope that our little grimoire inspires you to become the HWIC* of your own kitchen and continue to stir magickal intention into whatever you get bubbling in your cauldron. We'll call you for a kiki on the next full moon.

COOKING FROM THE GUT

Sometimes recipes can be more of a hindrance than a help. Maybe your "sear over medium-high heat" is different from ours. Or maybe the amount of cheese we ask for in one recipe is way more than you can handle! Use your gut instinct (pun intended) to make a dish that works for *your* palate. We call this intuitive cooking. It's the act of using recipes as guides (or using no recipe at all), tasting along the way, and letting your intuition tell you what to do next. It's not making it up as you go; it's more nuanced. It's doing what feels right. It's cooking with receptive energy.

The restaurant and food industry is generally dominated by active and even sometimes aggressive energy; there needs to be balance. Something to counteract the precision, the perfectionism, the rigidity, and rules. Intuitive cooking is taking your knowledge of cooking and technique and using it to cook from the heart.

Oh, hey there, it's me, Courtney!
You may notice several recipes in this book that are not based on anything close to my Anglo-European ethnicity. I grew up in Texas and have spent years living in New York City and Los Angeles and I also love to travel, so I am very lucky to have had access to a wonderful melting pot of flavors from all sorts of ethnicities, and they have all informed my cooking in one way or another.

To all the cooks and chefs who have influenced the recipes in this book: Thank you for sharing your food with me and for allowing me to sit at your tables. I hope only to honor you and your culture when I use your ingredients or techniques.

* HEAD WITCH IN CHARGE. A PLAY ON HBIC, WHICH MEANS . . . WELL, LET'S JUST SAY IT RHYMES.

WAYS TO USE THIS BOOK

You want magick and you wanna eat it. We're here to help. There are two ways into this book. The first is the traditional way: Look through the recipe titles, see what sounds good to you, and go make it. The second way is choosing by magick. That's a little more nuanced, so we'll spell it out for you.

DRAW A CARD

We think this one is the most fun, so it's up here at the top. You'll need a tarot deck. If you don't have one already, we highly suggest you pick one up. Obviously.

★ **Shuffle the deck** asking what energy would be most beneficial to you now. Keep shuffling until they feel "done" (or at least three times).

★ **Fan the cards out** on a table. This is a VERY satisfying move to master. You'll feel like a witchy croupier. It's wonderful.

★ **Draw a card.** Run your nondominant hand a couple of inches above the fanned-out cards. See if it feels pulled anywhere. Follow that pull. If you don't feel anything, just pick the one that's winking at you.

★ **Find your card's recipe** in this book and make it! And if you end up with something you're not in the mood for, take a peek at which magickal ingredients it uses and check the index to find other recipes that use those ingredients. Or be creative and use them as a starting point for your own experimentation.

CHOOSE A SPECIFIC CARD

If you are familiar with the Tarot and you know what energy you want to call in, by all means pick up the phone! And by "pick up the phone" we mean go to that page in this book and make that recipe.

CAST A SPELL

Want some help putting together a truly magickal meal? We got you. You'll find a selection of spells—recipes grouped together for their magickal and culinary qualities— for nine common themes (e.g., Creativity, Empowerment, Romantic Love) on page 175. We highly suggest checking these out. You'll learn a little about how tarot cards work together and a lot about what tastes great together, too.

BROWSE INGREDIENTS

Lastly, you can simply check out the Magickal Ingredient Pantry (page 12), look for some energy that sounds good, and consult the index to find what that ingredient has gotten into.

MAGICKAL INGREDIENT PANTRY

This is by no means a comprehensive list of all foods and spices with magickal properties. The world of kitchen magick is a vast wonderland with roots in cultural traditions from all across the globe. We encourage you to explore this world and we offer the magickal ingredients used in this book as a starting point. Each ingredient is listed here with the properties we intended to tap into with our recipes. As you gather more experience and knowledge, we hope you will add to this list, making it the seed of your very own personal kitchen grimoire. Oh, and if the ingredient is tricky to find, we've added tips on where you can source it; otherwise you can assume it's available at the grocery store or on the World Wide Web.

SALT ★ THERE IS ONE MAGICKAL INGREDIENT THAT IS SO COMMON, WE DIDN'T LIST IT OUT. BUT IT IS SO POWERFUL, WE CAN'T NOT TALK ABOUT IT: SALT.

SALT IS USED FOR CASTING PROTECTIVE CIRCLES FOR MAGICKAL WORKINGS, TO PURIFY AND CLEANSE RITUALISTICALLY IN BATHS, AND IN THE SPIRITUAL PROTECTION OF THE HOME. IT IS A MAJOR PLAYER IN BOTH THE WORLD OF MAGICK AND THE WORLD OF COOKING. WHENEVER YOU USE IT, KNOW THAT YOU ARE BANISHING A LITTLE EVIL FROM YOUR MOUTH.

ACHIOTE/ ANNATTO

PHYSICAL HEALTH AND HEALING

Achiote, also known as annatto, is a seed that is ground into a paste and used to lend a subtle, nutty flavor and also to impart a beautiful deep red color to food. You can find achiote paste in most grocery stores in the Latin foods section.

ALLIUMS

PURIFICATION, POWERFUL CLEARING

Alliums are a family of vegetables that includes onions, shallots, scallions, chives, garlic, and leeks.

★ **CHIVES** An herb with a mild onion flavor. Use only fresh chives for the recipes in this book, please!

★ **GARLIC** Sweet, wonderful garlic. We'll call for the entire head, halved horizontally, or for the individual cloves chopped or minced. Prechopped, jarred garlic exists, but please never use it. If you are working with the entire head and halving it horizontally (through the equator), leave the skins on to help the cloves stay connected. For minced garlic, it's best to use a garlic press or grate the cloves with a box grater or a Microplane.

★ **LEEKS** Be sure to wash them thoroughly, as leeks are typically quite sandy. To wash, submerge cut leeks in a bowl of water and let the dirt fall to the bottom. Scoop the leeks out of the water with a spider or slotted spoon. Don't worry about drying them for any of the applications in this book. The extra water steams and helps them soften without drying out.

★ **ONIONS** Red onions are slightly milder than the white and yellow variety. And while white and yellow are typically interchangeable, yellow onions do have a somewhat sweeter flavor.

★ **SCALLIONS** A much milder and smaller version of an onion. It has a white bulb and green stalk and all parts are edible. Refer to the recipe for instructions on which part to use.

★ **SHALLOTS** These alliums are like a cross between an onion and garlic, but a milder version of each.

ARTICHOKE

PERSONAL DEVELOPMENT

Artichokes come fresh, frozen, or canned, and each has specific applications. Typically speaking, fresh is best for when artichokes are the star attraction. Frozen or canned is best when the artichokes are part of a larger recipe, like Spinach Artichoke Roulade (page 33).

AVOCADO

PASSION, ATTRACTION, BEAUTY, BALANCING THE HEART

Be sure to get avocados with dark skin that gives a little when you press on it, which indicates ripeness. Don't you dare serve an unripe avocado.

BANANA

GRACE THROUGH CHANGE

When cooking with bananas, make sure they are ripe, otherwise whatever you are making won't actually taste like bananas. You'll know they are ripe when they are fragrant and the skins have brown spots all over them.

BAY LEAVES

PSYCHIC POWERS

All measurements in this book are for dried bay leaves. If you prefer to use fresh bay leaves, halve the amount listed, as fresh leaves are more pungent. Dried bay leaves can be found in the spice section of the supermarket.

BEANS

ABUNDANCE, GROWTH, PATIENCE

Beans come dried or canned. Use canned when you feel like phoning it in (which—let's be real—is totally okay), but for the Big Ol' Cauldron of Ranch-Style Beans (page 119), use dried. Yes, you will need to soak them overnight first, so plan for it!

BERGAMOT

JOY, TRUST, UPBEAT ATTITUDE

Bergamot is a type of sour orange, but unlike most orange varieties, it's generally not available in the grocery store. Lucky for us, it's a star ingredient of Earl Grey tea, which is how we infuse its magickal properties into our Fool recipe (Bergamot Baked Rice with Citrus and Honey, page 134). Earl Grey tea can be found in the tea aisle of the grocery store or in specialty tea shops.

BLACK PEPPER

ACTIVATES CONFIDENCE, EXPELS UNHEALTHY ENERGIES

Use freshly ground black pepper whenever you can. You can get a fancy pepper grinder and add the peppercorns yourself or grab one of those 2-in-1 black peppercorn/spice grinder thingamajigs from the spice aisle (you know what we're talking about).

BLACK TAHINI OR BLACK SESAME SEEDS

CLEARS NEGATIVE ENERGIES

Black tahini is made from toasted and ground black sesame seeds. It can be found in natural foods stores or online. Be sure to get a brand with no sugar or salt added.

BLACKBERRIES

ABUNDANCE, PROLIFERATION, HEALING

Be sure to use fresh blackberries, and if possible, get them in season at your local farmers' market.

BUTTERFLY PEA FLOWER

TRANSFORMATION, CONTENTMENT, CALM

This very magickal ingredient can be found in specialty tea shops or online. It comes as whole flowers or ground into a powder. We use the whole flowers for our Magician recipe (Butterfly Pea Flower Cinnamon Gimlet, page 137).

CAPERS AND CAPER BERRIES

LOVE, POWER

Capers and caper berries are usually found in jars in the pickle and condiment section of the supermarket. We use caper berries in the book, so be sure to grab those, not the smaller capers.

CARAWAY SEEDS

PROTECTION

Use whole caraway seeds for all purposes in this book. The protection caraway seeds offer provides a safe zone to explore topics and projects that require intense or prolonged periods of devotion.

CAYENNE PEPPER

ACTION, MOTIVATION, PASSION

Cayenne pepper rides the fine line between pleasant warmth and overwhelming scorch. Its heat level is tolerable (to most), yet still packs a punch. This is the level of energy it brings—enough to get you really going, but not so much that you'll burn out. See more chiles on page 15.

CELERY

MENTAL ACUITY, INTUITION, ARDOR

Celery is easily found in the produce section of the supermarket. Don't mistake the ubiquity of celery for weakness. Sometimes the most powerful magick can come from the most common ingredients—I mean, hello! You saw the sidebar on salt on page 12, right?

CHERRIES

VENUSIAN VIBES, LOVE, DIVINATION

Use fresh cherries! Frozen fruit just doesn't achieve the same effect. Rainier and Bing are the two most common varieties of cherry and both will get the job done with flair.

CHICORIES

PATH OPENER, SUCCESS

The chicory family includes many varieties (such as radicchio, endive, and escarole) and all can be found in the produce section of the supermarket. Once you've flexed your magickal cooking muscle a bit, you may even want to explore brewed chicory root as a coffee substitute or a base for a warm winter cocktail.

CHILES

PASSION, VITALITY, DRIVE

We use a lot of chiles in this book, in many different forms:

★ **ANCHO CHILE POWDER** This powder is made from ancho chiles, which are dried poblanos. It can be found in the Latin section of the supermarket or in specialty spice stores.

★ **CHILI OIL** Chili oil can be found in the Asian section of the supermarket, but due to its recent rise in popularity, you can find a lot of delicious artisanal versions in specialty food shops or online. In fact, Courtney used to make it herself for a company she started a long time ago called Large Marge (RIP Large Marge).

★ **CHILI POWDER** Chili powder comes in two main forms—dark and light—and is usually a blend of dried chiles and other spices, like garlic powder and cumin. Dark chili powder has more depth and it's what we prefer to use.

★ **FRESH CHILES** The chiles used most often in this book are jalapeños and serranos. They have slightly different flavor profiles, so don't use them interchangeably (but if you're in a pinch you totally can). The Fresno pepper is a mild red chile. For our purposes, poblano, Hatch, or Anaheim chiles can be used interchangeably for large green chile, but try to use Hatch if possible.

★ **GOCHUGARU** Gochugaru is finely flaked Korean red chile, often used in kimchi. It can be found in Asian supermarkets or online.

★ **GUAJILLO CHILES** These are the whole, dried form of the mirasol pepper and are commonly used in Mexican cooking. They can be found in the Latin section of the supermarket or online.

★ **RED PEPPER FLAKES** Also called chile flakes, these are the little red flakes of crushed-up chile peppers you get on the side when you order a pizza. They can be found in the spice section of the grocery store.

★ **TAJÍN** Tajín is a brand of chile-lime salt made in Jalisco, Mexico, that's great to rim glasses with or use on fresh fruit. It can be found in grocery stores, usually in the beverage aisle near the alcohol mixers, or sometimes in the produce section.

CILANTRO

PERSONAL CONNECTION

If you are the type of person who hates cilantro because it tastes like soap, feel free to omit it or substitute parsley. Look for fresh cilantro in the produce section of the grocery store because we use both the leaves and the stems in our cooking.

CINNAMON

MAGICK, SELF-MASTERY, CONNECTION TO ELEMENTS

We use cinnamon sticks and ground cinnamon in this book. This is one item that is just as great for dressing spell candles as it is for eating. Just a tiny sprinkle on top of a candle will fire up magickal abilities!

CLOVE

ATTRACTS ABUNDANCE, CLEARS AND ELEVATES VIBES

We use whole and ground cloves. If you love the smell of cloves, sleep with a little sachet of them by your bed or under your pillow to soak in the energy while you sleep.

COCOA

HEART OPENING, AMPLIFIES DIVINE LOVE

Always use high-quality chocolate—whether it's solid chocolate or cocoa powder—as it will affect the result of the dish. Any grocery store worth its weight should have some good options.

COCONUT

HONESTY, PATIENCE, SPIRITUAL PURITY

We use coconut in the form of sweetened coconut cream, which can usually be found in the beverage section of the grocery store, next to the alcohol mixers.

CUMIN

FIDELITY, PREVENTS THEFT, EXPELS NEGATIVITY

All recipes in the book call for ground cumin. You can buy it already ground or buy the whole seeds and grind 'em at home.

DANDELION

PHYSICAL, EMOTIONAL, AND SPIRITUAL CLEANSING AND PURIFICATION

When in season, dandelion greens can be found in the produce section of the grocery store or, better yet, at your local farmers' market.

DILL

ENHANCEMENT OF INTELLECT

Use only fresh dill for the recipes here. Got a problem you're having trouble solving? Draw a bath and add salt to clear the energy. Add a few sprigs of fresh dill to sharpen your understanding. Lean back, close your eyes, and let the answer float in.

EGGPLANT

ABUNDANCE, SUCCESS, FINANCIAL GAIN

There are lots of different eggplant varieties and they are all delicious. For the purposes of this book, we use the commonly found Italian eggplant.

ELDERFLOWER

EASES FEAR AND ANXIETY, PHYSICAL HEALTH

We use sweet, aromatic elderflower liqueur in this book. It can be found in most liquor stores or wine shops.

FENNEL

RITUAL, POTENCY, CREATION

You can use all parts of the fennel plant— the seed, the bulb, and the fronds. We use all three in our recipes here. The bulb and fronds come as a set and can be found in the produce section of the grocery store. The whole seeds can be found in the spice section.

FLAXSEED
HEALS PHYSICAL AND EMOTIONAL WOUNDS

Flaxseed comes as whole seeds or ground into a meal. We use the meal version in our Banana Flaxseed Muffins (page 171). It can usually be found in the baking section of the grocery store, next to all the alternative flours.

FRANKINCENSE
DIVINE CONNECTION, PROTECTION, ELEVATED VIBRATION

Frankincense is made from the resin of the tree *Boswellia sacra* and has been used in Ayurvedic medicine for hundreds of years, in Chinese medicine for over 2,000 years, and in religious ceremonies for at least 5,000 years. And yes, you can eat it! Look for frankincense oil in the essential oil section of your grocery store.

GINGER
CONFIDENCE, POWER, BENEVOLENCE

For sliced or finely grated fresh ginger, the skin should be always be removed first, then the root cut on a diagonal into ¼-inch-thick slices or grated on a Microplane. To remove the skin, use a peeler or scrape it off with the back of a knife or edge of a spoon.

Dried, ground ginger can be found in the spice section of the supermarket. Do not substitute ground ginger for any fresh ginger in this book, please and thank you.

GRAPEFRUIT
MENTAL CLARITY, INVIGORATION

Grapefruit is a large citrus fruit that can be found in the produce section of the grocery store. If you want that grapefruit feeling outside the kitchen, pick up some grapefruit essential oil to wear as a fragrance or add to a room mister.

HONEY
ETERNAL HOPE, LONGEVITY, SWEETNESS

Use any kind of honey you like. It can usually be found in the baking aisle or with all the jams, jellies, and bread.

HORSERADISH
URGENCY, POTENCY, PURIFICATION

We use prepared horseradish in this book, but if you prefer, you can get fresh horseradish root in the produce section of the grocery store. To use it, peel the skin and grate it on a Microplane or the small holes of a box grater.

JUNIPER BERRY
REPELS GHOSTS, BREAKS CURSES

Whole juniper berries can be found in the spice section of the grocery store.

LAVENDER
CALMING TO ALL LEVELS OF BEING

Use fresh or dried lavender. Dried can be found in specialty tea shops and often at your crunchier grocery stores. Fresh lavender might be found growing wild in your neighbor's backyard. (We do not condone stealing your neighbor's lavender, though.)

LEMON
LONGEVITY, BONDING, PURIFICATION, CLARITY, HONESTY

Always use freshly squeezed lemon juice, never bottled. Most recipes in this book ask for specific lemon juice measurements, either by the tablespoon, ounce, or cup. When purchasing, keep in mind that 1 small lemon usually yields about 3 tablespoons or 1½ fluid ounces of juice when squeezed with a hinged citrus press.

Preserved lemons are becoming easier to find in grocery stores, but they can also be found in Asian or Middle Eastern markets.

LICORICE ROOT
SAFETY, SECURITY, SHELTER

Licorice root can be found in most specialty tea shops or natural foods stores. It can be really hard to break up with your hands, and even harder to cut with a knife. Do your best, no one is going to judge you.

LIME
FIDELITY, ATTRACTION, PROTECTION

Always use freshly squeezed lime juice, never bottled. Most recipes in this book ask for specific lime juice measurements, either by the tablespoon, ounce, or cup. When purchasing, keep in mind that 1 lime usually yields about 2 tablespoons or 1 fluid ounce of juice when squeezed with a hinged citrus press.

MARJORAM
STRENGTHENS LOVE

When you eat what you've cooked with marjoram, you are enhancing the love you have for yourself as well as the love you share with your tablemates. The fresher the marjoram, the better.

MINT
EXTRASENSORY PERCEPTION, ELEVATES MOOD

Use only fresh mint for the recipes in this book. In addition to the magickal properties listed here, mint has been used for hundreds of years as a digestive aid. What elevates your mood faster than settling an upset stomach?

MITSUBA
COLLABORATION, COMFORT

Mitsuba is a Japanese herb that is kind of like parsley but has a piney flavor. It's like eating a pine tree in herb form. Look for it in Asian supermarkets. It's insanely delicious.

MUSHROOMS
PERSPECTIVE, CONNECTION

Mushrooms come in all shapes and sizes, most of which can be found in the produce section of the grocery store, or even better, at your local farmers' market.

MUSTARD
MENTAL ACUITY, ASTRAL TRAVEL

We call for four different forms of mustard in this book—Dijon, grainy, mustard seeds, and mustard powder. Traditional Dijon is the smooth, lighter yellow, spicy kind. Grainy mustards are darker and "old style" with the whole mustard seeds still in them. Both of these can be found in the condiment section of the grocery store. Mustard seeds and mustard powder (which is ground mustard seeds) can be found in the spice section.

NUTMEG
EXPANSION, GROWTH, PERSONAL DEVELOPMENT

Find nutmeg in the spice section of the grocery store. Buy it whole and grate it with a Microplane. Use preground nutmeg only if you must!

OLIVES
PEACE, SYMPATHY, BALANCE

Every grocery store's best kept secret? The olives from the antipasti bar. There is usually an assortment and they are always good. Fancy olives are also available at many specialty wine and cheese shops. Buy jarred olives in the condiment or canned section of the grocery store. Green Castelvetrano olives are great. They are mild, firm, and delish.

ORANGE

We use blood, mandarin, and navel oranges in this book. Unless otherwise noted, use navel oranges.

OREGANO

BEAUTY, LOVE, HAPPINESS

Oregano comes fresh and dried. If you have a cold, steeping fresh oregano in hot water makes a great immune-boosting tea. If you require a more robust solution, you can find oil of oregano capsules in most natural foods stores.

PAPRIKA

CREATIVITY

Paprika is a type of ground pepper, but it has its own magickal property. It comes smoked, sweet, or hot. We use smoked and hot in this book, but feel free to sub in sweet paprika for hot if you are averse to spice.

PARSLEY

THOUGHT, COMMUNICATION

Use only fresh Italian flat-leaf parsley for the recipes here. Because of its connection to planet Mercury, parsley influences intellect and communication, but it also has a strong history of use for protection and purification.

PECANS

MENTAL CLARITY, ABUNDANCE, LONGEVITY

Pecans come halved or in pieces. They can be found in the bulk section, the baking section, or the produce section of the grocery store. Look for unsalted unroasted pieces for the recipes here.

PINEAPPLE

LUCK

We use fresh pineapple and pineapple juice. Fresh pineapple can be found in the produce section. The juice can be found in the juice aisle.

POMEGRANATE

DIVINITY, TRAVEL BETWEEN WORLDS

Whole pomegranate can be found in the produce section of the grocery store and pomegranate juice lives in the juice aisle. You can use either for our High Priestess recipe (Pomegranate Julep, page 138).

POTATOES

GROUNDING, CONNECTION TO EARTH, GROWTH

Potatoes come in all shapes and sizes. For our purposes, we use fingerlings, russets, tots, and sweet potatoes. All of them can be found in the produce section of the grocery store. (Except the tots. You'll find those on the freezer aisle.) For sweet potatoes, use any kind you like, but just know that our favorites are the Japanese variety.

PUMPKIN

INTUITION, REFLECTION, INTROSPECTION

If you want to roast your own pumpkin and puree it for our Moon recipe (Pumpkin Corn Bread, page 167), go ahead, we won't stop you. But using canned pumpkin puree will be easier and more consistent. Canned pumpkin is available year-round and can usually be found in the baking aisle or with the canned goods.

RADISHES

PROTECTION AGAINST CURSES, NEGATIVE THINKING

Radishes come in many varieties, all of which are okay to use here. They can be found in the produce section of the grocery store or, even better, at your local farmers' market.

ROSE

HIGHEST EXPRESSION OF LOVE

We use rose water for the Empress card (A Rose Is a Rose Is a Rosé Punch, page 141). It can usually be found in the international section of the grocery store. If not, you'll definitely find it in Middle Eastern grocery stores or online.

ROSEMARY

CLEANSES AND PROTECTS THE HEART

Use only fresh rosemary for the recipes in this book. The rosemary salt you'll make as part of our recipe for The Devil (Rosemary Salt(ines), page 160) doubles as an excellent bath soak. Toss in a few whole sprigs to feel extra witchy.

SARSAPARILLA

PROTECTION, HEALTH, LUCK

Sarsaparilla is a woody root often used to make soft drinks. It can be found online or at specialty tea and spice stores. Look for root cut and sifted sarsaparilla.

SASSAFRAS

PROTECTION, LOVE, PROSPERITY

Sassafras is a bark—you may recognize the flavor as root beer. It can be found online or at specialty tea and spice stores. Be sure to get sassafras root bark.

SESAME OIL

CLEARS EVIL

Use toasted sesame oil. It has much more flavor and depth than the untoasted kind. It can be found in the Asian section of the supermarket.

SICHUAN PEPPERCORNS

PASSION, VITALITY, DRIVE

These aren't peppercorns at all! They are actually the seeds from the prickly ash plant and they are what makes your mouth tingle when you eat Sichuan food. They can be found in Asian supermarkets, at specialty spice shops, or online.

STONE FRUIT

SENSUALITY, SWEETNESS, AFFECTION

While some have slightly varying magickal associations, all stone fruit carry the energy of physical expression of love to some degree, peaches being the most potent. Stock up on nectarines, plums, mangoes, cherries, and dates, too.

STRAWBERRIES

LOVE, DIVINITY

The best time and place to buy fresh strawberries is in the height of their season at the farmers' market. Though it's best to keep strawberries chilled in the fridge, take them out and let 'em warm to room temp before serving, They're much more flavorful that way.

SUNFLOWER SEEDS

HAPPINESS, HONESTY, FERTILITY

Sunflower seeds can be found in the bulk section of grocery stores or produce section. Look for unsalted, toasted, and hulled seeds.

SWEET VIOLET
BALANCE, WELLNESS

We use crystallized sweet violet in this book. You can find it in specialty bake shops or online.

TURMERIC
CLEANSING, LUCK, SANCTITY

Turmeric is available fresh or ground. All our recipes call for ground turmeric, which will be in the spice aisle at your grocery store.

THYME
SHARPENS FOCUS, COURAGE UNDER STRESS

Use only fresh thyme for the recipes in this book. Thyme contains the natural antiseptic thymol and has a long history of medical use going all the way back to ancient Egyptian embalming techniques.

VANILLA
ATTRACTION, AGREEMENT, COMMUNION

Both vanilla beans and vanilla extract are available in the spice aisle of the grocery store. Beans are best used to steep in liquid. To prep a vanilla bean, slice it in half lengthwise, then use the back of your knife to scrape the seeds out. Drop the seeds and the pod into the liquid you are steeping it in.

EQUIPMENT AND TECHNIQUES

SHEET PANS

Many of our recipes call for sheet pans (aka rimmed baking sheets). Unless specified, you can use any size you want. Just note that a 9 x 13-inch sheet pan (also known as a quarter sheet) is specifically needed for some of our desserts.

BLENDER OR FOOD PROCESSOR

A high-powered blender is required for many of the recipes in this book. You don't need a super fancy one, but it can't be a dud, either, because you will be pureeing lots of stuff.

BOX GRATER

As a general rule of thumb, cheese should always be bought as a block and then grated. The pregrated stuff is coated with a substance that keeps it from clumping, but what you gain in ease, you lose in the quality of the melt. That said, no one is going to judge you if you are in a hurry and opt for the preshredded stuff.

CAST-IRON SKILLETS

Do yourself a favor and grab a medium (9- to 10-inch) and a large (11- to 12-inch) ovenproof cast-iron skillet. They are easier to clean than you think, and you'll be hooked in no time.

COOKING SPRAY

Get a can of this to grease your pans. It's quick and easy.

DUTCH OVEN

Everyone should invest in a 6- to 8-quart Dutch oven. (And we do mean invest, as they can be expensive.) You can fry, braise, or boil in it and they are generally very pretty to look at, so you can leave it out for display on the stovetop or counter.

GALLON ZIP-TOP FREEZER BAGS

This may sound strange, but you are gonna need these for quite a few recipes in this book. It's our secret weapon for easy-cleanup cooking. Be sure to wash and reuse them to prevent waste.

GARLIC PRESS

A garlic press is a quick and easy way to mince garlic. It also helps keep your fingers from smelling garlicky because you won't have to hand-chop it.

GIANT ICE CUBE TRAY

Get one of these to level up your cocktail game. The large cube melts more slowly than regular ice, so it doesn't water down the drink and it keeps it colder longer.

HINGED CITRUS PRESS

Get one of these to juice lemons, limes, and other small citrus fruits. You'll get more juice with a press than you would juicing by hand, plus it catches any seeds that might pop out of the fruit and into your dish. You can also use this tool to juice pomegranates and cherries!

ICE CREAM MAKER

For the best result with the Buttermilk Ice Cream (page 105), you'll need an ice cream machine. An ice cream attachment for a stand mixer works well, too.

MALLET

Also referred to as a meat tenderizer or pounder, mallets are the things that look kind of like a hammer, with one flat side and one prickly side.

INSTANT-READ THERMOMETER

You'll need a meat thermometer to measure the internal temp of meat or the temp of oil for frying. They can be found online or even at the supermarket.

MICROPLANE

You'll need this handy tool to grate citrus zest, parmesan cheese, and ginger.

MORTAR AND PESTLE

You can use a spice mill, food processor, or high-powered blender for most of the things you'd use a mortar and pestle for, but we highly recommend getting one anyway. There is something extra witchy about grinding your spices and ingredients together the old-fashioned way.

ROLLING PIN

Don't have one? No problem! You can also use a wine bottle.

STAND MIXER

This is not 100 percent necessary so long as you are okay with working those arm muscles by kneading dough, whipping egg whites, or creaming butter and sugar by hand. It's much faster and easier to use a stand mixer though. Once you get one, you'll wonder how you ever lived without it.

MINOR ARCANA

COOKING BY NUMBER (AND SUIT)

In the Tarot, the Minor Arcana gets into the details of our daily lives. These cards give insight into and guidance on what motivates us, how we behave, and our attitudes on particular subjects and situations. They can show us where we are and invite us to take certain steps to get closer to where we'd like to be.

Each suit has ten numbered cards and four court cards. The numbered cards give us nuanced versions of the energy of their elemental suit. Cups provide guidance on emotion (the realm of Water), Swords are linked to intellect and communication (the realm of Air), Wands center on creativity and instinct (the realm of Fire), and Coins represent our physical world, home, and finance (the realm of Earth). Numbers add a layer of symbolism onto each suit—from the pure power of the Aces to the seasoned experience of the Tens—and these cards reflect their elemental energies in different ways. The court cards (Page, Knight, Queen, King) all have two elemental energies at play, one for their suit and one for their title. They teach us how these energies look when they interact.

As you explore the Minor Arcana through tarot readings and our recipes, try to find examples from your own life that relate to the energies described. See if you can map out your life experiences according to the cards. When you start to move through life recognizing these energies as they come up, you'll be well on your way to being a full-fledged tarot reader.

To achieve ultimate kitchen witch status, fire up your cauldron and get cozy with the recipes that follow. Each of the Minor Arcana recipes is led by the elements and numbers described above. These dishes are full of magickal ingredients and you'll find food grouped by type: Swords/Air focus on poultry, Wands/Fire on meats, Cups/Water focus on seafood, and Coins/Earth on veggies. Desserts populate the stations of each suit's royal family, the court cards.

These recipes represent one way to interpret tarot cards into food. Once you get your bearings, we invite you to go off-book and explore different ways to bring this guidance into your life and body.

SWORDS

AIR ★ POULTRY

INTELLECT, COMMUNICATION, TRUTH

Swords carry the power of Elemental Air. When we engage in debate, contemplate our options, or have moments of clarity, we can thank the gift of Air. Learning to manage this power in our lives lets us analyze beliefs, form our own, and find our purpose. Air is the bridge between the inner and outer worlds, translating abstract messages from instincts and feelings into language, allowing us to communicate our needs and desires.

We'll be asking some fine feathered friends to join us as we explore the various expressions of Air in the Tarot. The numbered cards will kick off the party with poultry done ten ways, followed by the court cards each singing their own praises in the form of desserts. So, get your aquamarine jewelry polished up and your opinions sharpened. It's time to let that sparkling wit take flight.

ACE OF SWORDS

ACCEPTING THE GIFT OF AIR

The light bulbs are going off left and right. Ideas you've been bouncing around for years suddenly come into focus. Clarity opens and you can see the truth of every issue that's confused you. Trust it. Take it all in, write it down. Accept this information now, while it is offered. If you don't and the moment passes, it may be some time before you gain these insights again.

Said to boost immunity and improve digestive health, chicken broth is used as a cure for lung and sinus problems, the common cold, and even hangovers. We're just interested in helping you realize one of the world's great truths: Buying premade chicken broth is crazy because it is *so* easy to make yourself.

MAGICKAL INGREDIENTS: GARLIC AND ONION (SEE ALLIUMS)

CHICKEN BROTH

BACK POCKET BASIC —— MAKES ABOUT 4 CUPS

This broth recipe involves boiling a whole chicken along with its bones to yield a bunch of delicious shredded meat and skin, which you can use in the Chicken Tortilla Soup for the Witchy Soul (page 37), Chicken Skin Carbonara (page 41), or the Giant Banh Mìs (page 48).

No need to wash the chicken first; just stick it in the pot along with any innards it came with. And don't season the finished broth; you can add salt and pepper to taste once you know what you are going to use it for.

If you already have chicken bones on hand from roasting a chicken, you can easily make a broth without boiling a whole chicken first. Simply add the bones to a stockpot, cover them with water by an inch or two, add some aromatics like onion or maybe a bay leaf if you're feeling crazy, and simmer it on low until the stock is flavorful, delicious, and reduced.

1 whole chicken (4 to 5 pounds)

1 large white or yellow onion, peeled and quartered

1 head garlic, halved horizontally

1. Place the chicken breast-side down in a large stockpot. Add the onion and garlic and cover completely with water. Bring the water to a boil over medium-high heat, then reduce the heat to low, cover, and simmer until the internal temperature of the chicken is 155°F (it will continue cooking to 165°F once it comes out of the pot), about 30 minutes.

2. Remove from the heat and transfer the chicken to a bowl or cutting board.

3. When the chicken is cool enough to handle, use your hands to remove the skin and all the meat from the bones. Return all the bones to the stockpot, along with any juices left in the bowl. Store the chicken meat in an airtight container in the fridge for up to 4 days or in the freezer for up to 4 weeks.

4. Bring the broth to a simmer over medium-high heat, reduce the heat to low, partially cover, and cook until the liquid has reduced by about one-third, about 3 hours. Remove any large bones and strain the broth through a fine-mesh sieve. Store in an airtight container in the fridge up to 4 days or in the freezer for up to 1 month.

TWO OF SWORDS
MAKING DECISIONS

The decisions you make now are leading you to something big. Even the ones that seem insignificant offer glimpses into the future you are already moving toward. Pay attention to the choices you make every day and see if you can find a pattern. When you do, be ready for a make-or-break situation to present itself.

To ease any stress of making all those decisions, our Two of Swords recipe does not ask you to choose between an appetizer or a main—you get both in one dish. As a bonus, artichoke encourages personal development, so you'll be sure to keep heading in the direction that's best for you.

MAGICKAL INGREDIENTS: ARTICHOKE, GARLIC (SEE ALLIUMS),
BLACK PEPPER, RED PEPPER FLAKES (SEE CHILES)

SPINACH ARTICHOKE ROULADE

MAIN —— SERVES 3 OR 4

You're about to make one big batch of spinach artichoke dip, bake half, and use the rest in a chicken roulade. Yes, this recipe is literally a double dipper.

SPINACH ARTICHOKE MIXTURE

8 ounces full fat cream cheese, softened

¼ cup sour cream

1 (16-ounce) bag frozen spinach, thawed, drained, and finely chopped

1 (14-ounce) can artichoke hearts, drained and roughly chopped

4 ounces fresh mozzarella cheese, shredded

¼ cup finely grated parmesan cheese

1 teaspoon minced garlic

¼ teaspoon red pepper flakes

Kosher salt, to taste

ROULADES

2 boneless, skinless chicken breasts (about 1½ pounds total)

Kosher salt and freshly ground black pepper

½ cup all-purpose flour

1 large egg, beaten

1¼ cups panko bread crumbs

Canola or vegetable oil, for shallow-frying

FOR SERVING

Tortilla chips

Hot sauce

1 lemon, cut into wedges

1. Preheat the oven to 325°F.

2. **PREPARE THE SPINACH ARTICHOKE MIXTURE:** In a large bowl, combine all ingredients. Add salt to taste. Transfer half the mixture to a half-quart baking dish and set aside.

3. **PREPARE THE ROULADES:** Working with one at a time, place a chicken breast between two sheets of parchment or wax paper and use a mallet to pound to ¼ inch thick.

4. Season the chicken breasts with salt and pepper, then lay each one on a separate sheet of plastic wrap. Divide the remaining spinach artichoke mixture and spread it evenly over each breast. Starting at the narrower end of the chicken, roll it up tightly, then wrap it in the plastic wrap. Pull the plastic taut and twist each end like a Tootsie Roll to tighten. Let the rolls set in the fridge for 30 minutes.

5. Spread the flour in a large shallow bowl. Add the egg to a second bowl and the panko in a third. Unwrap the chicken and dredge each roulade in the flour and then the egg, turning to coat fully. Shake off any excess, then dredge in the panko, again, shaking off any excess.

6. Set a wire rack in a sheet pan. Pour ½ inch of oil into a large skillet or Dutch oven and heat over medium-high until the oil begins to shimmer. Add the roulades and cook until they are golden brown, about 5 minutes per side. Set them on the wire rack.

7. Transfer the dip and the chicken to the oven and bake until the roulades reach an internal temperature of 155°F, 15 to 20 minutes.

8. Remove the roulades from the oven and let rest for 15 minutes. If needed, let the dip continue baking until it browns slightly and bubbles up around the sides. Cut the roulades into 1-inch-thick rounds and serve with the dip, tortilla chips, hot sauce, and lemon wedges.

Just when you thought you'd finally narrowed down the possibilities, another viewpoint shakes up your contemplation. While conflicting opinions can quickly fill a room (or a head) with stress and tension, they don't have to. Take a step back, take a deep breath, and allow this new perspective to inform your view, not shatter it.

To help you slow down, fry up a batch of our chicken wings. You'll have a good chunk of time to kill while they're soaking in marinade. Use it to meditate, take a long bath, go for a run, or all three. These wings are going to be dripping in honey, so you're sure to come out of this whole mess with a clear mind and a hopeful heart.

MAGICKAL INGREDIENTS: CAYENNE, HONEY

SOUTHERN FRIED HOT HONEY WINGS

SNACK —— SERVES 3 OR 4

Although they are messy as hell to eat, these wings are surprisingly not that messy to make. The trick is using 1-gallon freezer bags for everything, thus keeping the mess locked inside the bag, not on your counter or floor. And you can wash and reuse the bags, so there is no unnecessary waste.

Once they are all fried, place the chicken in a single layer on a large plate or platter and make it rain honey all over them. Finish with a dousing of hot sauce and you'll have some seriously savory, sweet, sticky, and perfectly piquant wings on your hands. Literally. Did we mention how messy these are to eat?

HOT TIP ★ IF YOU DON'T HAVE A THERMOMETER TO TEMP THE OIL, WE HIGHLY SUGGEST YOU GET ONE. IF YOU REFUSE, YOU CAN TEST THE OIL BY DROPPING A LITTLE BIT OF THE FLOUR COATING INTO IT. ONCE IT STARTS TO SIZZLE, THE OIL IS READY. IF THE WINGS BEGIN TO DARKEN TOO QUICKLY, TURN THE HEAT DOWN. IF IT TAKES THEM FOREVER TO BROWN, TURN THE HEAT UP.

1 large egg, beaten

1 cup buttermilk

1 teaspoon kosher salt

1 teaspoon granulated sugar

1 teaspoon cayenne pepper (optional)

3 pounds chicken wings (about 24 pieces)

Canola or peanut oil (about 2 quarts), for deep-frying

2 cups all-purpose flour

¼ cup cornstarch

¼ cup rice flour

1 tablespoon seasoned salt, such as Lawry's

Garlic salt, such as Lawry's

Honey, for serving

Louisiana-style hot sauce (such as Crystal), for serving

1. In a 1-gallon zip-top bag, combine the egg, buttermilk, salt, sugar, and cayenne. Add the chicken wings. Put that bag in another gallon freezer bag (in case the first one springs a leak). Shake the bag around and put it in the fridge for at least 4 and up to 8 hours. Give the bag a shake every hour or so to make sure the chicken stays evenly coated and brined.

2. Preheat the oven to 250°F.

3. Pour 3 inches oil into a large Dutch oven and heat to 350°F. Place a wire rack on a sheet pan and set aside.

4. In a 1-gallon zip-top bag, combine the flour, cornstarch, rice flour, and seasoned salt and shake to combine. One at a time, take the wings out of the bag of brine and allow any excess brine to drip off. Then add the wings to the flour mixture, seal the bag, and shake well to coat.

5. Working in 3 batches, use tongs to gently place the wings directly from the bag into the hot oil. Fry the wings until the breading is a deep golden brown and crispy, about 5 minutes. Transfer the fried wings to the rack on the sheet pan and season to taste with garlic salt. Keep warm in the oven while you cook the remaining wings.

6. Drizzle generously with honey and hot sauce to serve.

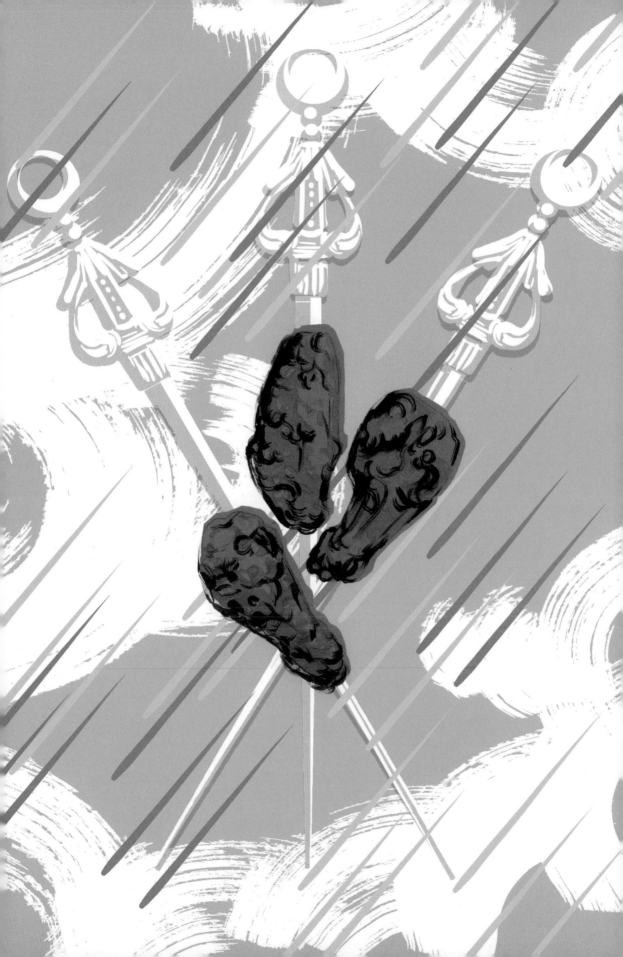

Forming a personal value system takes a lot of effort. You take in piles of information from your surroundings, sift through it, try some values on for size, get uncomfortable, find your boundaries, and finally see which principles are most important to uphold. It's a rite of passage we go through over and over in life, so it's best to cozy up to it.

Nothing is more cozy than chicken soup (we asked the entire world, and everyone agreed). Sit down with a bowl of this chicken tortilla soup and reflect on how great it feels to be standing solid in your convictions. The scallions and garlic will clear out any last bits of doubt while lime keeps you true to your word.

MAGICKAL INGREDIENTS: SCALLION (SEE ALLIUMS), GARLIC (SEE ALLIUMS), LIME, GUAJILLO CHILE (SEE CHILES), CILANTRO, ONION (SEE ALLIUMS), AVOCADO

CHICKEN TORTILLA SOUP
FOR THE WITCHY SOUL

MAIN —— SERVES 4 TO 6

This soup is based on the traditional Mexican *sopa de Azteca*, which, in its most basic form, is a chicken and tomato broth flavored with chiles and topped with fried tortilla strips. If you ever have the chance to go to Mexico and taste an authentic *sopa de Azteca*, it will change your life.

Canola or peanut oil, for shallow-frying

4 corn tortillas, cut into ¼-inch-wide strips

Kosher salt

6 guajillo chiles, stemmed and seeded

6 cups chicken broth, store bought or homemade (page 32)

1 small bunch cilantro, separated into stems and leaves

1 large white or yellow onion, peeled and quartered

6 garlic cloves, peeled

2 whole peeled tomatoes (from a can), plus 2 tablespoons of the juice

Kosher salt, to taste (about 2 teaspoons)

1½ teaspoons ground cumin

¼ cup fresh lime juice

2 teaspoons sugar

2 cups shredded cooked chicken, store-bought or homemade (see Chicken Broth, page 32)

FOR SERVING

1 avocado, sliced

Sliced scallions

Sour cream

Crumbled queso fresco

1 lime, cut into wedges

1. Pour ½ inch oil into a medium pot and heat over medium-high until it begins to shimmer. Add the tortilla strips and fry until they are lightly browned and crispy, 3 to 4 minutes. Drain on paper towels and season with salt.

2. In a medium skillet, dry-toast the guajillo chiles over medium-high heat until covered with dark brown spots, about 1 minute per side.

3. Fill a pot three-quarters full with water. Add the guajillos and bring to a boil over medium-high heat. Reduce the heat to low and simmer until the chiles are soft, about 30 minutes, submerging them as needed throughout cooking.

4. Meanwhile, in a separate large pot, bring the chicken broth to a simmer over medium-high heat. Add the cilantro stems, remove from the heat, cover, and set aside. Chop the cilantro leaves and set aside.

5. Transfer the softened chiles to a blender. Add the onion, garlic, tomatoes, tomato juice, cumin, and 3 tablespoons of the chili cooking water. Puree on high.

6. In a large skillet, cook the chile-tomato puree over medium-high heat, stirring occasionally, until darkened and reduced to about 1½ cups, about 10 minutes.

7. Remove the cilantro stems from the chicken broth and discard. Whisk the reduced puree, lime juice, and sugar into the broth, then stir in the shredded chicken. Bring the mixture to a simmer over medium-high heat, then remove from the heat.

8. Serve family style with the tortilla strips, chopped cilantro leaves, avocado, scallions, sour cream, queso fresco, and lime wedges on the side.

FIVE OF SWORDS
FIGHTING ANXIETY

There's no use sugarcoating it—this card radiates anxiety. The classic "racing thoughts, can't trust what you say, nothing you say lands how you mean it" kind. The last thing you need to add to a chaotic Air situation is more Air, so cease any attempts to "figure it out" *immediately*. The only thing to do is breathe and invite the anxiety to pass. You can help it find the door a bit quicker with a salty brine and juniper berries.

    The main magick of these duck legs is that they soak in salt—the master clearing and protecting agent of the metaphysical realm—for a long time. But it's the banishing power of those juniper berries that really keeps the stress away.

MAGICKAL INGREDIENTS: JUNIPER BERRIES, BAY LEAVES, LEMON, GARLIC
(SEE ALLIUMS), BLACK PEPPER, SHALLOTS (SEE ALLIUMS), MARJORAM

CONFIT A DUCK!

MAIN —— SERVES 3 TO 4

Everyone should know how to confit a duck. It's easy, impressive, and delicious. The cool thing is you can confit duck legs way in advance, keep them fully submerged in the fat that you cooked them in for up to a month, and then crisp them to order.

    Speaking of fat, confiting uses a lot of it at the start and you end up with even more of it at the end. Use the leftovers to either make more duck confit or to sauté anything that you want to make extra tasty. Most butcher shops will have duck fat available for sale, but if you have problems sourcing it, you can substitute chicken fat or even olive oil.

HOT TIP ★ DON'T SKIP THE RINSING STEP! OTHERWISE YOUR DUCK LEGS WILL BE VERY, VERY SALTY. TRUST US, WE LEARNED THIS THE WAY WE LEARN EVERYTHING: THE HARD WAY.

1 tablespoon black peppercorns

1 tablespoon juniper berries

2 bay leaves

¼ cup kosher salt

6 whole duck legs

2 cups duck fat

4 shallots, peeled and halved

8 sprigs fresh marjoram or thyme

1 head garlic, halved horizontally

1 lemon, quartered

1. With a mortar and pestle, mini food processor, or spice grinder, process the peppercorns, juniper berries, and bay leaves until crushed. Pour the mixture and salt into a 1-gallon zip-top bag, give it a shake, then add the duck legs to the bag, seal, and shake well to coat. Place the bag of salted duck legs in the fridge for 18 to 24 hours to cure, tossing every few hours.

2. Preheat the oven to 300°F.

3. In a small saucepan, heat the duck fat over medium heat until just melted.

4. Discard the cure and rinse the legs and pat dry. Arrange the legs snugly, skin-side up, in a 12-inch Dutch oven. Using a paring knife, poke holes all over the skin, being careful not to perforate the meat below.

5. Add the shallots, marjoram, garlic, and lemon to the Dutch oven, then pour the fat over until the legs are barely covered. Transfer to the oven and bake uncovered until the meat is tender, 3 to 3½ hours. Keep an eye on the legs. If they aren't fully submerged and begin to get very browned, cover the pot.

6. Remove from the oven and let cool in the pan for 20 minutes. Transfer the shallots to a small bowl. Squeeze the garlic and lemon into the same bowl and use a spatula or fork to mash into a chunky paste.

7. To serve, remove the legs from the fat and crisp them, skin-side down, in a large skillet over medium-high heat, until they are browned, 2 to 3 minutes. Serve slathered with the garlic-lemon mash.

SIX OF SWORDS
FINE-TUNING THE MESSAGE

There's no shame in changing your mind. In fact, the worst thing you can possibly do with a belief is hold it so tightly that you become rigid. You know what happens to rigid trees in the wind, right? They break. Be like a palm—flexible with a great head of hair. Making adjustments to your communication style doesn't make you inconsistent; it makes you smart and accommodating.

Another thing that makes you smart: using the chicken skin you saved from making that chicken broth way back at the Ace of Swords (page 32)! Plus, parsley is associated with planet Mercury, named for the god of communication, so you're getting excellent support for refining your Air element manifestations.

MAGICKAL INGREDIENTS: PARSLEY, BLACK PEPPER, RED PEPPER FLAKES (SEE CHILES)

CHICKEN SKIN CARBONARA

MAIN —— SERVES 2 OR 3

This recipe is preeeeeeeeettty cool. It's like a classic carbonara, except it uses chicken skin and schmaltz instead of the traditional guanciale (or pancetta) and lard. We won't mix the chicken skins into the pasta, either; we'll just sprinkle them on top so they stay exxxtra crispy. I'm sure someone somewhere will hate us for breaking tradition, but hey, sometimes traditions were meant to be broken (see above re: fine-tuning the message).

Most butchers will have chicken skins at the ready, but you can also buy a package of skin-on chicken breasts or thighs, remove the skins and use that. Or save the skin from Chicken Broth (page 32). You'll cook them kind of like you are cooking bacon, slow and low so the fat renders and they get extra crispy.

HOT TIP ★ ALWAYS SALT PASTA WATER GENEROUSLY. THE WATER SHOULD TASTE JUST A HAIR LESS SALTY THAN THE OCEAN. YES, THAT'S A LOT OF SALT! BUT IT'S THE SECRET TO MAKING DELICIOUS PASTA.

4 ounces raw or boiled chicken skin (see page 32), thinly sliced

Kosher salt and freshly ground black pepper

1 large egg

4 large egg yolks

2 cups grated pecorino cheese (about 5 ounces), plus more for serving

16 ounces spaghetti

Chopped fresh Italian parsley, for serving

Red pepper flakes, for serving

1. In a large nonstick skillet, heat the chicken skin over low heat until the fat renders and the skins get extra crispy, about 15 minutes.

2. Transfer the chicken skins to paper towels and season with salt and pepper. Measure out 2 tablespoons of the fat from the skillet and set aside to cool to room temperature. Discard any remaining fat.

3. In a large bowl, whisk the whole egg, egg yolks, and pecorino until combined, then whisk in the cooled chicken fat.

4. Bring a large pot of salted water to a boil over medium-high heat. Once the water is boiling, add the spaghetti and cook according to the package directions. Using tongs or a pasta fork, transfer the cooked noodles to the egg mixture. Stir immediately to combine. Taste and add salt and pepper as needed.

5. Serve topped with the chicken skins, parsley, pepper flakes, and more grated pecorino.

HOT TIP ★ FOR A THINNER SAUCE, ADD PASTA WATER, A FEW TABLESPOONS AT A TIME, TO THE MIXTURE UNTIL YOU GET TO A CONSISTENCY THAT YOU LIKE.

Even the most confident among us come across occasions when we hesitate to speak our minds. Maybe we don't know the people in the room very well or we doubt just how well informed our opinion really is. When that hesitation becomes habitual, we need a little push to get past it. This energy helps you free yourself of the mean inner critic and instead make friends with the kind, helpful one.

Mustard and paprika are the magickal stars of this show, boosting mental faculties and creativity to make it *fun* to share your point of view. Plus, you get to practice speaking up for what you believe in, taking a stance on the controversial subject of BBQ sauce on pizza. It's a real win-win.

MAGICKAL INGREDIENTS: MUSTARD, PAPRIKA, GARLIC (SEE ALLIUMS), CUMIN, BLACK PEPPER, ONION (SEE ALLIUMS), CILANTRO, JALAPEÑO (SEE CHILES)

BBQ CHICKEN FRENCH BREAD PIZZAS

MAIN —— SERVES 4

These. Pizzas. Are. Insanely. Delicious. And the best part is, this procedure can be used as a blank slate to make any other kind of French bread pizza you like. Make one with sausage and mushroom. Or try a few with a different, wacky kind of cheese, like Fontina.

Before adding the chicken, you'll char it on one side. Don't worry about flipping the chicken thighs or cooking them all the way through. They'll finish cooking on the pizza while it's in the oven.

As for the tomato sauce, if you want your pizzas extra saucy, use all of it. If you prefer less sauciness, use anywhere between ¼ and ⅓ cup per pizza and save the leftovers for another use. Oh, and if you are averse to spice, you can use pepperoncini or roasted bell peppers instead of jalapeños. Or omit the peppers altogether.

HOT TIP ★ THESE HOLD UP IN THE FREEZER, TOO. YOU CAN MAKE THEM ONE DAY, FREEZE THEM, AND REHEAT THEM IN THE OVEN (FOR ABOUT 30 MINUTES AT 375°F) WHENEVER YOU FEEL LIKE A SNACK.

TOMATO SAUCE
1 (14-ounce) can whole peeled San Marzano tomatoes

2 tablespoons extra-virgin olive oil

1 teaspoon kosher salt

BBQ CHICKEN
1 tablespoon canola oil

1 pound boneless, skinless chicken thighs

Kosher salt and freshly ground black pepper

½ cup barbecue sauce, store-bought or homemade (recipe follows)

PIZZAS
2 loaves French bread (12 to 14 inches long)

3 cups shredded mozzarella cheese

½ small red onion, thinly sliced

About 20 slices pickled jalapeños, store-bought or homemade (see Pickled Veggies, page 113)

¼ cup chopped fresh cilantro

Barbecue sauce, store-bought or homemade (recipe follows), for serving

1. **MAKE THE TOMATO SAUCE:** In a blender, combine the tomatoes, olive oil, and salt and process until the tomatoes have completely broken down.

2. **MAKE THE CHICKEN:** In a large skillet or grill pan, heat the oil over high heat until shimmering. Season the chicken with salt and pepper. Add the chicken to the skillet and sear for 3 minutes, until charred. Remove from the skillet and let cool for 10 minutes. Once cool, cut the chicken into 1-inch chunks and transfer to a large bowl. Pour in the barbecue sauce and toss to coat.

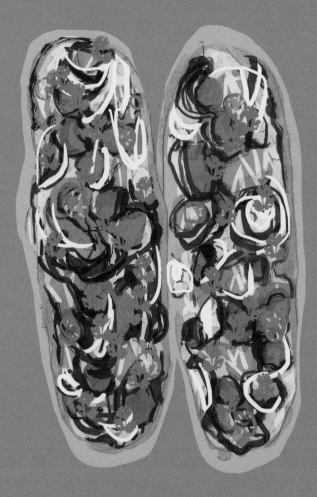

3. Preheat the oven to 425°F.

4. **ASSEMBLE THE PIZZAS:** Split the loaves lengthwise and separate the two halves. Scoop out a little bit of the bread in the middle of each to make room for all the toppings. Lay the loaves, cut-side up, on two sheet pans. Divide the tomato sauce among the loaves and spread the sauce out in an even layer. Top each with ¾ cup shredded mozzarella, then add the chicken, sliced onion, and pickled jalapeños.

5. Bake the pizzas until the cheese melts and browns on top, 10 to 15 minutes. Remove from the oven and let cool for about 5 minutes.

6. To serve, garnish with cilantro and more barbecue sauce and slice into 2-inch-wide rectangles.

BODACIOUS BBQ SAUCE
MAKES ABOUT 1½ CUPS

1 cup ketchup

⅓ cup vegetable or chicken broth, store-bought or homemade (pages 32 and 108)

¼ cup apple cider vinegar

2 tablespoons Worcestershire sauce

1 tablespoon light brown sugar

1 tablespoon grated white onion

1½ teaspoons minced garlic

2 teaspoons smoked paprika

1½ teaspoons mustard powder

¼ teaspoon ground cumin

¼ teaspoon kosher salt

In a small saucepan, stir together the ketchup, broth, vinegar, Worcestershire sauce, brown sugar, onion, garlic, smoked paprika, mustard powder, cumin, and salt. Bring to a simmer over medium-high heat, then reduce the heat to low and cook uncovered for 5 minutes, or until fragrant. Store in an airtight container in the fridge for up to 2 weeks.

EIGHT OF SWORDS
FORMING A WORLDVIEW

This isn't your first rodeo. Your journey through life has taken you on a ride through enough places, relationships, and situations that you've developed a pretty keen ability to read a room. So keen, in fact, that a holistic worldview all your own is coming into focus. The lens through which you see the world informs all your decision-making and how you think about yourself and others.

While it can shift over time, what you're putting together should be big enough to work for you now and well into the future. Get creative and push your boundaries. Cinnamon and ginger are great allies in that quest to open your imagination.

MAGICKAL INGREDIENTS: CLOVE, CINNAMON, GINGER, TURMERIC, CAYENNE, GARLIC (SEE ALLIUMS), CILANTRO, ONION (SEE ALLIUMS), LEMON, OLIVES, PARSLEY

ODE TO
CHICKEN TAGINE

MAIN —— SERVES 4 TO 6

The history of tagine is long and varied, with the earliest mention of this cooking style found in the pages of *One Thousand and One Nights*. Traditionally, tagine is prepared in a cooking vessel called a . . . tagine! We use a Dutch oven here. Don't forget to serve this with a bowl of couscous on the side.

HOT TIP ★ WHEN YOU RETURN THE CHICKEN THIGHS TO THE POT YOU MAY NEED TO SQUISH THEM IN. TRY TO MAKE SURE THEY GET MOSTLY COVERED WITH THE LIQUID TAGINE MIXTURE.

2 tablespoons unsalted butter

½ cup sliced almonds

8 bone-in, skin-on chicken thighs

Kosher salt and freshly ground black pepper

2 tablespoons extra-virgin olive oil

1 large yellow onion, diced

1 teaspoon cayenne pepper

1 teaspoon ground turmeric

¼ teaspoon of each, ground: allspice, cinnamon, cloves, coriander, ginger

6 garlic cloves, chopped

1 tablespoon tomato paste

2 cups chicken broth, store-bought or homemade (page 32)

1 (28-ounce) can whole peeled tomatoes, crushed

1 cup green olives, crushed

1 cup dates, pitted and roughly chopped

3 tablespoons finely chopped preserved lemon

1 tablespoon chopped cilantro

1-inch piece fresh ginger, finely grated

FOR SERVING

Chopped Italian parsley

Chopped cilantro

Scallions, thinly sliced

1 lemon, cut into wedges

1. Preheat the oven to 350°F.

2. In a small skillet, melt the butter over medium-low heat. Add the almonds and cook until they are golden brown and toasted, about 6 minutes. Remove the skillet from the heat.

3. Pat the chicken thighs dry and season with salt and pepper. In a large Dutch oven, heat the olive oil over medium heat until shimmering. Working in batches, add the chicken skin-side down and sear until browned, about 4 minutes per side. Transfer the chicken to a plate and let rest.

4. Pour off all but 2 tablespoons of fat from the Dutch oven. Add the onion, cayenne, and ground spices, and stir to combine. Cook over medium heat until the spices are fragrant and the onion is soft, 4 to 5 minutes. Stir in the garlic and tomato paste and cook until the tomato paste darkens, about 2 minutes more.

5. Add the chicken broth, crushed tomatoes, olives, dates, preserved lemon, cilantro, fresh ginger, and the buttery toasted almonds and stir to combine. Return the chicken to the Dutch oven. Increase the heat to medium-high and bring to a simmer.

6. Cover and transfer to the oven. Bake for 40 minutes, until the sauce is infused with flavor and the chicken is cooked through. Remove from the oven and let cool for 10 minutes.

7. Serve topped with parsley, cilantro, and scallions, with lemon wedges for squeezing.

NINE OF SWORDS
APPRECIATING DIFFERENCES

The real test of whether someone truly believes in their views is if they tolerate the views of others. For the person who has faith in their beliefs, differing positions are not a threat to be extinguished, but topics to discuss. Welcome these discussions with open arms. They will contribute to your own intellectual development and allow you to find others who enjoy exploring ideas as much as you do.

Staying true to your values while allowing your beliefs to evolve is a noble pursuit, if difficult. Lemon promotes fidelity to support the former, while fennel encourages the latter by offering energetic protection and personal vitality. You'll find both in this recipe for braised chicken legs.

MAGICKAL INGREDIENTS: LEMON, FENNEL

BRAISED CHICKEN GAMS
WITH PEA TENDRILS AND FENNEL

MAIN —— SERVES 4

This is an extremely simple dish with the light, subtle flavors of pea tendrils, fennel, and lemon playing off each other in beautiful harmony. They are in love and they aren't afraid to show it.

Be sure to use pea *tendrils*, not pea shoots. If you can't find pea tendrils, use a cress—watercress, garden cress, or upland cress are all great options. And if you can't find any of those, arugula or spinach will work.

3 tablespoons extra-virgin olive oil

4 whole chicken legs, thighs and legs attached

Kosher salt and ground white pepper

4 large shallots, finely chopped

1 small bulb fennel, finely chopped, fronds chopped and reserved

1 cup dry white wine

1 lemon, halved

2 tablespoons unsalted butter

1 bunch pea tendrils

1. In a large Dutch oven, heat the oil over medium heat until shimmering. Season the chicken legs with salt and white pepper. Working in batches, add the chicken, skin-side down, and sear until the skin is crisp and browned on one side, about 5 minutes. Flip and cook 5 minutes more, until the other side is browned, too.

2. Remove the chicken, reduce the heat to medium-low, and add the shallots and chopped fennel bulb. Cook until softened and the shallots are translucent, about 7 minutes.

3. Add the wine and bring to a simmer, scraping any browned chicken from the bottom of the pan. Return the chicken and any resting juices to the Dutch oven. Place the lemon halves in the Dutch oven and spoon the vegetable mixture over the chicken. Reduce the heat to low, cover, and simmer until the chicken has reached an internal temperature of 160°F, about 30 minutes.

4. Remove the chicken from the Dutch oven and let rest. Increase the heat to medium-high and cook for 5 minutes to thicken the sauce. Remove the Dutch oven from the heat, squeeze in the lemon juice, and add the butter and 2 tablespoons chopped fennel fronds. Taste and add salt as needed.

5. To serve, spoon the sauce over the chicken and top with pea tendrils.

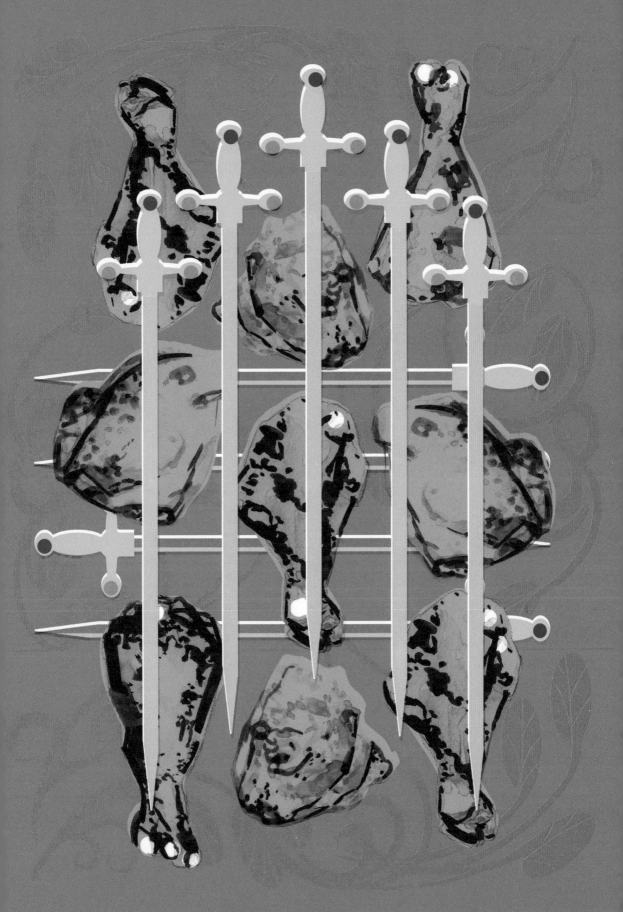

TEN OF SWORDS
TAKING RESPONSIBILITY

It's all coming back to you now. The late-night talks, furious journaling, heated confrontations, and apologies of varying levels of sincerity. Some of the opinions you defended so urgently have fallen away while others look far more significant now than they did at the time. The views you've outgrown are just as important to your development as the values you've held on to.

It's time to begin the process again. Will you get informed on politics, art, science, the history of balloon art in the Americas? You've got a moment to consider it now, but you're going to get hungry. Make a giant sandwich and make it a banh mì.

MAGICKAL INGREDIENTS: LEMON, GARLIC (SEE ALLIUMS), TURMERIC, CILANTRO, JALAPEÑO (SEE CHILES)

GIANT, BANH MÌS
WITH GARLICKY TURMERIC AIOLI

MAIN —— SERVES 3 TO 4

The Vietnamese banh mì might be the best sandwich ever invented in the history of the world (it's a close race, considering the Giant Roast Pork Sandwiches, page 72). The ingredients vary, but they most often include pâté, some sort of meat, pickled carrots and daikon, hoisin sauce, cilantro, cucumbers, and mayonnaise—all sandwiched inside a fluffy Vietnamese baguette.

If you can't find a Vietnamese baguette, use any bread with a thin, flaky crust and soft insides. You'll need two 14-inch loaves. Or four 7-inch ones. It doesn't really matter—you'll just need 28 inches of bread.

Make the pickled carrots and daikon and chicken liver pâté ahead of time so all you'll have to do is assemble the sandwich. You can also omit the daikon and just buy pickled carrots from the store and shred them in a food processor or on a box grater.

HOT TIP ★ TO PROPERLY CLEAN CHICKEN LIVERS, SOAK THEM IN COLD WATER FOR 15 MINUTES, THEN USE A KNIFE TO TRIM OFF ANY MEMBRANES, FATTY BITS, OR GREEN-HUED PARTS.

TURMERIC AIOLI

½ cup mayonnaise

¼ teaspoon minced garlic

1 tablespoon fresh lemon juice

½ teaspoon ground turmeric

PÂTÉ

2 tablespoons extra-virgin olive oil

1 large shallot, finely diced

½ pound chicken livers, cleaned and trimmed

¼ cup bourbon or brandy

Kosher salt and freshly ground black pepper

6 tablespoons (3 ounces) cold unsalted butter, chunked

BANH MÌ

2 crusty Vietnamese baguettes (14 inches long)

10 ounces shredded cooked chicken, store-bought or homemade (see Chicken Broth, page 32)

2 Persian (mini) cucumbers, halved and cut into thin matchsticks

2 cups pickled carrots and daikon (recipe follows)

1 large jalapeño (optional), seeded and thinly sliced

½ cup fresh cilantro leaves

½ cup hoisin sauce

Sriracha, for serving

1. **MAKE THE TURMERIC AIOLI:** In a small bowl, whisk together the mayonnaise, garlic, lemon juice, and turmeric.

2. **MAKE THE PÂTÉ:** In a large skillet, heat the olive oil over medium heat until shimmering. Add the shallot and cook until soft and translucent, about 3 minutes. Add the livers and bourbon, season with salt and pepper, and cook until soft and browned, 4 to 5 minutes.

3. Transfer the livers to a blender or food processor. Add the cold butter and process on high until a smooth paste forms, about 1 minute. Taste and add salt and pepper as needed. Scrape the pâté into a small bowl and cover with plastic wrap. Refrigerate until chilled, at least 2 hours.

4. Preheat the oven to 400°F.

5. ASSEMBLE THE BANH MÌS: Split the bread in half lengthwise and place on a baking sheet. Toast the bread until crisp on the edges, 4 to 5 minutes. Remove the bread from the oven. Spread the aioli evenly on the bottom half of each loaf, then add the chicken, cucumbers, carrots and daikon, jalapeño slices (if using), and cilantro. Spread the hoisin and pâté on the top halves of each loaf. Press the loaves together and slice each sandwich into thirds.

6. Serve with a side of Sriracha . . . and a bottle of cold white wine.

PICKLED CARROTS AND DAIKON

1 cup shredded carrot
1 cup shredded daikon
1 cup vinegar
1 tablespoon granulated sugar
2¼ teaspoon kosher salt

1. Follow the procedure for pickling (see recipe on page 113).

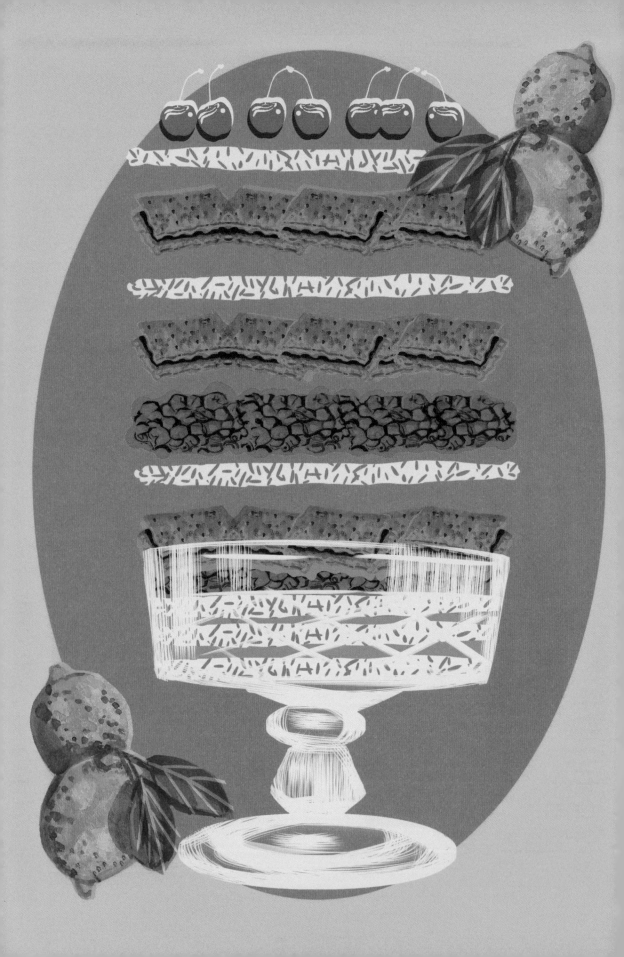

PAGE OF SWORDS

EARTH OF AIR ★ EXPANDING VOCABULARY

The words you've been using to describe your world have worn out their welcome. Take inventory of the most common things you say and consider their accuracy; are they coloring your perception in an unhealthy way? Explore new ways of expressing how you see the world around you. You'll find that your attitudes shift with your language.

To give that new view a rosier hue, eat cherries. They have a long history of use in love spells, ensuring you'll gravitate toward language that describes what you adore. Dress them up for a garden party in this cherry lime icebox cake. The lime and vanilla are excellent co-conspirators.

MAGICKAL INGREDIENTS: CHERRIES, LIME, VANILLA

CHERRY LIME ICEBOX CAKE

DESSERT —— SERVES 8

Part cake, part Key lime pie, and part cherry limeade, this recipe is the one to make for a warm summer soirée, when cherry season is at its peak. The basic premise is to layer cookies with whipped cream, put it in the icebox (aka refrigerator), and let the cookies soak up the moisture from the whipped cream overnight. By that time, the cookies will have softened into a cake-like texture and from there, you slice and serve.

There is but one downside to this cake: At some point, the graham crackers will become oversaturated with the lime and cherry juice and they'll turn to total mush. You'll have about a 48-hour window before this happens, so EAT UP.

HOT TIP ★ UNLESS YOU ARE USING A VERY TALL PAN, YOUR ICEBOX CAKE WILL LIKELY COME UP OVER THE EDGE. IT'S OKAY, KEEP BUILDING IT UP, IT STAYS PUT AND WON'T TOPPLE OVER.

1 pound cherries

¼ cup granulated sugar

2 teaspoons grated lime zest

½ cup fresh lime juice

1 (14-ounce) can sweetened condensed milk

2 cups heavy cream

2 teaspoons vanilla extract

¾ cup powdered sugar

¼ teaspoon kosher salt

23 graham cracker sheets

1. Pit and roughly chop half the cherries. In a small bowl, combine the chopped cherries and the granulated sugar and set aside to macerate for 1 hour. Lightly press on the cherries to help release their juices. Drain off the excess liquid and discard.

2. In a large bowl, combine the lime zest, lime juice, and sweetened condensed milk and set aside.

3. In a stand mixer fitted with the whisk, combine the heavy cream, vanilla, powdered sugar, and salt. Whip the cream until medium peaks form, 3 to 4 minutes. Do not overbeat! Fold the whipped cream into the lime and condensed milk mixture.

4. Spread ¼ cup of the lime cream in the bottom of a trifle dish or an 8 × 8-inch baking dish. Add an even layer of graham crackers on top, breaking them as needed to fit. Evenly spread ¾ cup of the lime cream on top of the graham crackers, then repeat with another layer of graham crackers and ¾ cup of lime cream. Layer half of the macerated cherries on top of the lime cream, then layer another round of graham crackers, lime cream, and the remaining cherries. Finish with two more rounds of graham crackers and lime cream.

5. Cover the cake loosely with plastic wrap and refrigerate for at least 4 hours. To serve, top with a pile of the remaining whole cherries.

KNIGHT OF SWORDS

FIRE OF AIR ★ SPEAKING OUT

Something needs to be said and you're going to be the one to say it. The fire of conviction is burning in your throat, pushing you to give voice to long ignored issues, personally and globally. Take one more moment to frame your words in a way that maximizes their impact and conveys your passion without undermining the message. Then, let it out loud and proud!

Truly, nothing says "loud and proud" like ice cream on fire. The sheer gall of a frozen treat engulfed in a ball of flame is awe-inspiring. Will it burn you or give you a brain freeze? BOTH. So, look out and look alive.

MAGICKAL INGREDIENTS: CINNAMON

BAKED ALASKA
WITH CINNAMON TOAST CRUMBS

DESSERT —— SERVES 8

In its truest form, a Baked Alaska is ice cream and cake, covered with a browned meringue. This recipe uses cinnamon toast bread crumbs instead of cake, and they are layered throughout for crunch. You might end up with extra crumbs because the amount you'll need depends on the diameter of the bowl you use. Our favorite ice cream combo is Buttermilk (page 105), strawberry, and mint chip, but you do you!

HOT TIP ★ YOU CAN BROWN THE MERINGUE VIA BLOWTORCH OR OVEN. IF YOU WANT TO USE A BLOWTORCH, SIMPLY RUN THE TORCH OVER THE ALASKA DIRECTLY AFTER COVERING IT IN MERINGUE AND SERVE.

CINNAMON TOAST CRUMBS

2 sticks (8 ounces) unsalted butter, melted

2 cups plain dried bread crumbs

1 cup sugar

1½ teaspoons ground cinnamon

¼ teaspoon kosher salt

BAKED ALASKA

3 pints ice cream of your choosing

4 large egg whites, at room temperature

¾ cup sugar

⅛ teaspoon cream of tartar

1. MAKE THE CINNAMON TOAST CRUMBS: Preheat the oven to 325°F.

2. In a large bowl, combine the butter, bread crumbs, sugar, cinnamon, and salt. Transfer the crumbs to a baking sheet and bake for 30 to 40 minutes, tossing halfway through, until the crumbs are browned and fragrant. Let cool to room temperature.

3. ASSEMBLE THE BAKED ALASKA: Remove one pint of ice cream from the freezer and let soften. Mist a narrow 3-quart bowl with cooking spray, then line the bowl with plastic wrap. Put the ice cream in the bowl and press into the bottom using the back of a spoon. Cover the top of the ice cream with enough of the cinnamon toast crumbs to make a layer ¼ inch thick and lightly press them into the ice cream. Place the bowl in the freezer for at least 30 minutes.

4. Repeat with the next 2 pints of ice cream, making the final layer of crumbs ½ inch thick, and freezing for 30 minutes after each layering. Cover the Alaska with plastic wrap and place in the freezer for at least 4 hours.

5. Line a sheet pan with parchment paper and place it, along with the platter you plan to serve the Baked Alaska on, in the freezer.

6. In a stand mixer, fitted with the whisk, whip the egg whites on high until frothy. Add the cream of tartar and continue whisking until soft peaks form. Slowly add the sugar and continue whipping until peaks are shiny, glossy, and firm.

7. Remove both the Alaska and the sheet pan from the freezer. Remove the plastic wrap from the top of the Alaska and invert it onto the frozen sheet pan. Remove the outer plastic wrap and, working quickly, use a spoon to coat the Alaska in the meringue, making sure not to leave any exposed ice cream. Return the Alaska to the freezer for at least 2 hours more.

8. Preheat the oven to 500°F.

9. Bake the Alaska until the meringue is lightly browned, 3 to 4 minutes. Transfer the Alaska to the frozen serving platter immediately after removing it from the oven, then slice and serve.

QUEEN OF SWORDS

WATER OF AIR ★ EXPRESSING THE HEART'S TRUTH

Your heart has been waiting patiently for this moment to arrive. She has kept quiet while you calculated, negotiated, and strategized, using your words as armor to fortify your position. Now the barricades are coming down and emotional perspectives are flooding out. Revel in their unabashed fervor.

This chocolate soufflé is a perfect representation of this state. Cocoa, revered for its heart-opening and love-promoting powers, is joined with actual air in the form of whipped egg whites. See? If intellect and emotion can play nicely in a soufflé, they can play nicely inside of you.

MAGICKAL INGREDIENTS: COCOA, VANILLA

MAKE-AHEAD
CHOCOLATE SOUFFLÉ
WITH AMARO SAUCE

DESSERT —— SERVES 4

You can make these soufflés in advance and bake them to order later. If you aren't familiar with the ins and outs of making soufflés, this is a HUGE deal.

There are many different kinds of amaros to choose from. For the sauce, be sure to stick with one that is sweet and stay away from anything that is bitter.

Remember, when buttering and sugaring the insides of the ramekins, make sure every inch is covered or your soufflés won't rise properly!

LITERAL HOT TIP ★ WHEN COOKING ALCOHOL THERE IS A CHANCE IT WILL IGNITE. IF YOUR AMARO SAUCE DOES, IT'S ALL GOOD. SIMPLY TURN OFF THE HEAT AND WAIT FOR IT TO BURN OFF.

Butter and sugar for the ramekins

BATTER

6 ounces chocolate (60% to 70% cacao), roughly chopped

1 tablespoon unsalted butter

3 large egg yolks

1 tablespoon amaro, such as Nardini

1 teaspoon vanilla extract

1 teaspoon kosher salt

5 large egg whites

⅛ teaspoon cream of tartar

½ cup sugar

AMARO SAUCE

½ cup amaro, such as Nardini

2 tablespoons sugar

1 tablespoon unsalted butter

1. Grease four 6-ounce ovenproof ramekins with butter and coat with sugar.

2. **MAKE THE BATTER:** Fill a pot halfway with water and bring to a simmer over medium-high heat. Reduce the heat to low. Add the chocolate and butter to a large metal bowl, then place the bowl on top of the pot and stir with a spatula until fully melted and combined. Remove the bowl from the heat and whisk in the egg yolks, amaro, and vanilla until combined. Set aside.

3. In a stand mixer fitted with the whisk, whip the egg whites on high until frothy. Add the salt and cream of tartar and continue whisking until soft peaks form. Slowly add the sugar and continue whipping until peaks are shiny, glossy, and firm.

4. Using the spatula, vigorously stir one-third of the meringue into the chocolate mixture until fully combined, then delicately fold in the remaining meringue in two batches until fully combined. Divide the batter among the ramekins, filling them all the way to the top, then scrape off the excess to create a smooth, flat surface that's flush with the top edge. Using a damp paper towel, wipe away any batter that spilled over the edges. Freeze the soufflés for at least 3 and up to 8 hours.

HOT TIP ★ IF YOU WANT TO BAKE OFF THE SOUFFLÉS IMMEDIATELY, PREHEAT THE OVEN TO 400°F AND BAKE THEM RIGHT AWAY FOR 10 TO 12 MINUTES.

5. Preheat the oven to 400°F. Place the frozen ramekins on a sheet pan and bake until they are puffed and browned on the top and edges, 23 to 25 minutes.

6. **MEANWHILE, MAKE THE AMARO SAUCE:** In a small saucepan, combine the amaro, sugar, and butter. Bring to a simmer over medium-high heat, reduce the heat to medium, and cook for about 5 minutes to thicken.

7. Remove the soufflés from the oven, then poke a hole in the center of each and pour over the sauce. Serve immediately.

KING OF SWORDS

Just the facts, friend. You're meticulously analyzing the situation to ensure every thought is aligned and truthful. No assumptions, no unfounded leaps of logic, no mistaking correlation for causation. You need a rock-solid intellectual foundation for your life plans to grow big and strong as you reach into the future. Pay attention to the subtle meanings of your words to avoid any misunderstandings down the line.

You will definitely not have to worry about any misunderstandings around the greatness of this bread pudding. Straightforward, honest, and uncompromising, it even demands to be made from airy croissants lest you doubt the sincerity of its elemental devotion. Use it as a litmus test for your confidants—if they don't like it, don't trust 'em.

MAGICKAL INGREDIENT: VANILLA, CINNAMON

CROISSANT BREAD PUDDING

DESSERT —— SERVES 8

Sometimes all you want is a classic, custardy bread pudding with just a hint of vanilla and cinnamon, and that's exactly what this is. Use croissants instead of plain bread for a richer, more buttery flavor, and make sure they are at least a day or two old so they soak up the creamy egg mixture.

You can certainly eat this bread pudding plain, but I much prefer a heavy drizzle of the amaro sauce used for the Make-Ahead Chocolate Soufflé (page 54) or, for a more playful version, a drizzle of the Root Beer Elixir Float (page 104). Plain ol' maple syrup or whipped cream would also be delicious.

3 cups whole milk

2 cups heavy cream

1¾ cups sugar

2 teaspoons pure vanilla extract

4 cinnamon sticks

1 teaspoon kosher salt

8 large eggs

14 stale croissants, torn into 1-inch chunks

1. In a large saucepan, combine the milk, heavy cream, sugar, vanilla, cinnamon sticks, and salt and bring to a boil over medium-high heat.

2. In a large bowl, whisk the eggs. Once the milk mixture boils, remove from the heat and slowly whisk into the bowl with the eggs, whisking constantly until combined.

3. Add the croissants to the bowl and push them down to the bottom. Let the mixture cool to room temperature, pushing the croissants down every few minutes. Cover the bowl tightly with plastic wrap and refrigerate for 6 hours or up to overnight.

4. Preheat the oven to 350°F. Grease a 9 × 13-inch baking dish.

5. Remove the mixture from the fridge and discard the cinnamon sticks. Transfer the mixture into the baking dish, and bake until the edges and top have browned, about 1 hour.

6. Serve warm or at room temperature.

WANDS

FIRE ★ MEATS

ACTION, INTUITION, CREATION

Wands carry the power of Elemental Fire, an energy that allows us to act on instinct, to sense something before we can know it, to create works of art and whole arcs of existence. Fittingly, Fire is the element that gives us magick, as magick at its most basic is creating something (an outcome, a protective shield) out of nothing. When you get a feeling about something, color outside the lines, or take action, that's the element of Fire activating in your life.

   This section will take you on a journey through the various personalities of the Wands. We'll first explore ten variations of the element of Fire on its own with meats dressed up ten different ways. Then we'll meet the court cards, personalities with elemental energies all their own that steer how they work with Fire. They're bringing the desserts. Now, pop a carnelian stone in your pocket, throw on some fast music and something orange, and let's go!

ACE OF WANDS
ACCEPTING THE GIFT OF FIRE

The power that fuels our will is being offered a major boost; reach out and take it. Trust your instincts. They'll get you where you want to go faster than the most carefully planned route ever could. There is no need to worry about unforeseen circumstances—if you encounter any, you'll improvise the perfect solution.

Listen to what your gut tells you about making this bone broth. We've given you a good outline, but it's up to you to fill in the details. We're certain you'll manage to stir your own magick into the pot.

MAGICKAL INGREDIENTS: BAY LEAF, ONION (SEE ALLIUMS)

BONE BROTH

BACK POCKET BASIC —— MAKES ABOUT 4 CUPS

There are about as many ways to make a bone broth as there are to bone, which is to say . . . LOTS. This way is simple and gets the job done. Let's call it the "missionary-style" recipe for bone broth.

You can either save up bones as you work your way through the meat dishes in this chapter, popping them in the freezer until you have enough to make broth, or buy bones straight from the butcher. Any bone'll do!

The broth technique is quite simple. All you need to do is roast the bones, throw them in a pot and cover them with water by an inch or two, add some aromatics, and simmer away, partially covered, until you are left with a deeply flavorful broth.

HOT TIP ★ KEEP IN MIND, THE TYPE OF BONE WILL AFFECT THE RESULT OF THE BROTH. TRY TO GO FOR A MIX OF MARROW BONES, KNUCKLE BONES, AND MEATY BONES LIKE OXTAIL FOR THE BEST RESULT.

4 pounds raw beef bones
2 tablespoons extra-virgin olive oil
1 large yellow or white onion, roughly chopped
1 bay leaf

1. Preheat the oven to 375°F.

2. Spread the bones out on a baking sheet and drizzle them with the olive oil. Roast them until the attached tissue starts to brown, about 25 minutes.

3. Add the onion, roasting until the onion becomes translucent and lightly browned, about 15 minutes more.

4. Transfer the bones and onion to a large stockpot. Add water until the bones are submerged and add the bay leaf. Bring to a boil over medium-high heat, then reduce the heat to low and simmer with the lid slightly ajar until the liquid is reduced by half, 3 to 4 hours. Skim the surface with a ladle as needed to remove and discard any foam.

5. Discard the bones. Then strain the broth through a fine-mesh sieve and discard any solids. Store in an airtight container in the fridge for up to 1 week, or in the freezer for 3 months.

TWO OF WANDS
CHOOSING A LANE

An unexpected fork in the road can be stressful or exciting depending on your perspective. The difference lies in whether you focus on what you are leaving behind or what you are moving toward. Take a moment to check in with your gut, pick a lane, and go. And don't look back.

To let you practice, we've got this simple cow~~boy~~-person steak. With chili oil lighting the fire of confidence to get the job done and sesame oil and salt to clear any negative thought out of the way, you'll be intuiting exactly when and where to pivot (and when that steak is perfectly done) in no time.

MAGICKAL INGREDIENTS: CHILI OIL (SEE CHILES), SESAME OIL, CILANTRO, PARSLEY, BLACK PEPPER

BONE-IN COWPERSON STEAK
WITH SESAME CHILI OIL

MAIN —— SERVES 2 OR 3

It doesn't matter whether you call it a bone-in rib eye, a cowboy/girl/person steak, or even côte de boeuf, this is always an impressive cut of beef and dang near impossible to mess up. You'll start this baby off in a skillet, getting it extra crispy on both sides, then finish it in the oven, but keep a watchful eye—this is where the overcooking hazard begins (the only way you can mess this up). Most people prefer to cook theirs to medium-rare, but if you prefer yours cooked to medium, nobody will judge you, especially not us.

You'll slice it into strips, drizzle a combo of chili oil and sesame oil all over the top (a cue taken from a favorite Korean BBQ spot in LA), and finish it with a dusting of big, flaky salt and a garnish of your choosing. Serve it up with a side of fried rice or some roasted vegetables. If you don't like spicy things, you can omit the chili oil and use all sesame oil, but don't skip this step!

2 tablespoons canola oil

1 bone-in cow~~boy~~-person steak, 2½ inches thick (about 2 pounds)

Kosher salt and freshly ground black pepper

3 tablespoons chili oil

3 tablespoons toasted sesame oil

Flaky salt, such as Maldon, for serving

Chopped cilantro or Italian parsley, for serving

1. Preheat the oven to 400°F.

2. In a large ovenproof cast-iron skillet or grill pan, heat the canola oil over medium-high heat. Season the steak liberally with salt and pepper. When the oil starts to shimmer, add the steak to the pan and sear it undisturbed on both sides until it is crusty and brown, about 5 minutes per side.

3. Transfer the pan to the oven and roast the steak to desired doneness: 20 minutes for medium-rare (a meat thermometer will read 125°F) or a few extra minutes for medium (a meat thermometer will read 130°F).

4. Remove the steak from the oven and rest it on a cutting board for 15 minutes. Meanwhile, in a small bowl, combine the chili oil and sesame oil.

5. Slice the steak against the grain into ¼-inch chunks. Drizzle the oil on top and garnish with the flaky salt and cilantro.

Even when there are perfectly good, worn-in roads available, sometimes you have to cut your own way. Unspoken information from inside yourself and from sources beyond is pointing you toward exploration. You might want to pack a bag. There's no telling how far this new direction will take you.

To fill up before hitting the road, practice choosing your own adventure with our beef short ribs. Direct the magick in this recipe by serving it with one of our side dishes. Focus the energy outward toward worldly accomplishment with the Six of Coins Smashed Sweet Potatoes (page 117) or inward with the solitary exploration of The Hermit Sauerkraut from Scratch (page 149). And even if you choose to brave the ribs alone, you'll have the protection of caraway seeds to keep you safe.

MAGICKAL INGREDIENTS: CARAWAY SEEDS, BLACK PEPPER, ONION (SEE ALLIUMS), MUSTARD, BAY LEAF

SLOW-BRAISED BEEF SHORT RIBS IN SAUERKRAUT
WITH SPICY MUSTARD

MAIN —— SERVES 4

This succulent short rib dish is a take on the classic German meal of brats braised in sauerkraut. The ribs cook in the liquid and give it a deep, umami flavor while the sauerkraut gets soft and cabbage-y. Which makes sense, because sauerkraut is made of 99.9 percent cabbage. You can certainly buy sauerkraut from the store, but if you have the time and desire, the Sauerkraut from Scratch (page 149) with licorice root was *made* for this recipe. If you choose to take this route, first of all, we love you, second of all, make sure to add a few chunks of the licorice root to the braising liquid. It adds depth, a little bit of sweetness, and an herbaceous, camphor-like quality.

3 tablespoons extra-virgin olive oil

3 to 3½ pounds bone-in beef short ribs

Kosher salt and freshly ground black pepper

1 medium yellow onion, diced

2 teaspoons mustard powder

½ teaspoon caraway seeds

2 cups chicken broth, store-bought or homemade (page 32)

2 cups sauerkraut drained, store-bought or homemade (page 149)

2 tablespoons grainy mustard, plus more for serving

1 bay leaf

1. In a large Dutch oven, heat the olive oil over medium-high heat. Season the short ribs with salt and pepper. When the oil is shimmering, add the ribs and sear until browned, about 3 to 4 minutes per side. Transfer the ribs to a plate and remove all but 2 tablespoons of fat from the Dutch oven. Reduce the heat to medium, add the onion and a pinch of salt, and sauté until just softened and translucent, about 5 minutes. Add the mustard powder and caraway seeds and cook 2 minutes more, or until fragrant.

2. Add the broth to the Dutch oven and scrape any browned bits off the bottom. Add the sauerkraut, grainy mustard, and bay leaf and stir to combine. Return the ribs to the Dutch oven and bring to a simmer over medium-high heat. Reduce the heat to low, cover, and simmer until the short ribs start to fall apart and the sauerkraut softens, 2½ to 3 hours.

3. Taste and add salt and pepper as needed. Transfer the short ribs to plates and ladle the sauerkraut and juices on top. Add a dollop of mustard and serve with a loaf of crusty bread on the side.

THIS RECIPE IS TRULY THE SOULMATE OF THE HERMIT SAUERKRAUT RECIPE ON PAGE 149. NOT ONLY ARE SHORT RIBS AND SAUERKRAUT MADE FOR EACH OTHER, THE INDIVIDUALISTIC HERMIT REALLY ENCOURAGES YOU TO GO YOUR OWN WAY. AND THE LICORICE ROOT IN THE KRAUT GIVES YOU ADDED SAFETY FOR THE ROAD.

FOUR OF WANDS
IMPROVISING STABILITY

Stay light on your feet and you won't feel the ground shifting beneath you. Remain flexible and nimble in all areas of life to feel grounded in the dynamic element of Fire. It's tricky, but you're well positioned to master this art form. Attach yourself to the process rather than the outcome and make sure you always have a plan B at the ready.

Take these green chile pork chops for example; while maintaining their status as a Southwest comfort food, they keep you on your toes, asking you to save the leftover sauce for another dish. Which dish? The witch dish! (Just kidding, that's every recipe in this book.) No matter what, you'll be protected by the magick of garlic, cilantro, and cumin.

MAGICKAL INGREDIENTS: CHILE, GARLIC (SEE ALLIUMS), CILANTRO, CUMIN, ONION (SEE ALLIUMS), LIME

GREEN CHILE PORK CHOPS

MAIN —— SERVES 3 OR 4

Nothing beats pork cooked in a green chile sauce. The citizens of the Southwest know it and now you do, too. Use a Hatch chile if they are in season, otherwise, poblano or Anaheim will work.

If you have a gas burner, you can char the peppers over the flame until the skin blisters (instead of broiling them in the oven). As a low-key pyromaniac, this is Courtney's preferred method.

The best part of this recipe (besides potentially getting to light things on fire) is all the leftover green chile sauce you'll have. Don't throw it away! Use it on the Queso Fundido (page 64) or the Crispy Ground Beef and Pickle Tacos (page 70), or on anything, really.

1 large Hatch green chile

1 large jalapeño

2 small tomatillos, husked and halved

1 small red onion, roughly chopped

4 garlic cloves, peeled

1 small bunch cilantro, stems and leaves separated

1 cup chicken broth, store-bought or homemade (page 32)

2 teaspoons kosher salt

1 tablespoon ground cumin

1 tablespoon dark chili powder

2 pounds bone-in pork chops, about 1½ inches thick

3 tablespoons extra-virgin olive oil

1 tablespoon fresh lime juice

1. Set the oven to broil.

2. Arrange the Hatch green chile and jalapeño on a sheet pan and broil until the skins are charred, about 5 minutes per side. Remove the peppers from the oven and immediately cover with foil. Let steam in the foil for 10 minutes or until cooled. Run under cold water to remove the skins, stems, and seeds.

3. Place the tomatillos cut-side down on the same sheet pan and broil until charred, about 10 minutes. Set aside to cool.

4. In a blender, combine the cooled tomatillos, red onion, garlic, cilantro stems, chicken broth, and half the roasted peppers and puree on high for about 30 seconds. Chop the remaining roasted peppers into ¼-inch dice and add them to the puree.

5. In a small bowl, combine the salt, cumin, and chili powder. Rub the mixture all over the pork chops. In a large cast-iron skillet, heat the olive oil over medium-high heat. When the oil is shimmering, add the pork chops and sear, undisturbed, until golden brown, about 4 minutes per side.

6. Pour the green chile puree into the pan and reduce the heat to medium. Simmer until the internal temperature of the pork reaches 140°F, 8 to 10 minutes. Transfer the pork chops to a cutting board and let rest for 15 minutes.

7. Meanwhile, increase the heat under the skillet to medium-high and cook the sauce for 5 to 7 minutes to thicken and reduce. Stir in the lime juice. Taste and add salt as needed

8. Slice the pork against the grain into ¼-inch-thick chunks and top with the sauce and cilantro leaves to serve.

FIVE OF WANDS
ACCEPTING POWERLESSNESS

When you find yourself unable to make progress in a situation no matter how hard you push, unable to hear your inner voice or find a creative solution, you're in a Five of Wands moment. Don't panic, they usually don't last long, but they are very frustrating if you try to fight them. All you can do is sit back and watch the show. You're gonna need a snack.

Fortunately, we have the World's Greatest Recipe for the World's Greatest Snack (official title patent pending). Queso Fundido has it all. It's substantial, it goes well with other snacks, and it's made of cheese. Whip up a batch to share or to devour in one sitting while waiting out the chaos.

FITTINGLY, FOR A CARD INDICATING AN ABSENCE OF MAGICK,
THERE ARE NO MAGICKAL INGREDIENTS IN THIS RECIPE.

QUESO FUNDIDO

SNACK —— SERVES 4 TO 6

Don't confuse this with the Tex-Mex cheese dip that is also called queso. This is queso *fundido,* which translates to molten cheese, and that is exactly what it is: a molten vat of gooey, melty glorious cheese. This version (as most do) also has sausage. Chorizo is our choice, but you can use breakfast, Italian, or even bratwurst. We're not here to tell you how to live your life, but chopped BBQ brisket would also be great in this. And if you want some Coins energy, use A Big Ol' Cauldron of Ranch-Style Beans (page 119) instead of any meat at all!

Serve this with leftover green chile sauce from the Green Chile Pork Chops (page 63), salsa, tortilla chips, and flour tortillas.

HOT TIP ★ TO SPICE YOURS UP EVEN MORE, CUT UP SOME ONION, GARLIC, OR PEPPERS AND SAUTÉ THEM IN THE SAUSAGE FAT BEFORE LAYERING THEM IN WITH THE CHEESE.

8 ounces fresh chorizo, or pork sausage of your choosing, casings removed

8 ounces Oaxaca cheese

8 ounces Monterey Jack cheese

Tortilla chips or flour tortillas, for serving

1. Preheat the oven to 400°F.

2. In a skillet, cook the sausage over low heat until it starts to release its fat. Increase the heat to medium-high and continue cooking until browned and crumbly, about 10 minutes, stirring occasionally. Drain the sausage on paper towels and set aside to cool slightly.

3. Meanwhile, grate both cheeses on the large holes of a box grater into a large bowl and toss to combine.

4. Spread half of the cheese in the bottom of an 8- or 9-inch square or round baking dish or ovenproof skillet. Spread half of the sausage evenly over the cheese. Layer on the remaining cheese and finish with the remaining sausage.

5. Bake until the cheese is melted and just starting to bubble around the edges, 8 to 10 minutes. Don't let it brown.

6. Serve immediately with tortilla chips or flour tortillas.

SIX OF WANDS
CELEBRATING CREATION

You've reached a level of skill in bringing projects to life that are worth shouting about. Through a combination of risk-taking, perfect timing, and fearlessly trusting your inner voice, you've gone further than you thought you could. Let that pride sink in with the lessons you learned along the way. But for now, revel in the moment.

Reveling is way more fun in a group, so invite some friends to join in. You can get this Yucatán-style lamb shoulder in the oven before they arrive to set yourself up for the ultimate "Oh, this? It was nothing!" host with the most moment. With bay leaves in the mix, you'll be giving your guests a boost of their own intuitive powers.

MAGICKAL INGREDIENTS: BAY LEAVES, OREGANO, LIME, GARLIC (SEE ALLIUMS), ORANGE, ACHIOTE/ANNATTO, CILANTRO, ONION (SEE ALLIUMS)

YUCATÁN-STYLE LAMB SHOULDER TACOS

MAIN —— SERVES 8 TO 12

This is an ode to the Yucatán dish of *cochinita pibil*, but, instead of *cochinita* (baby pork), we'll use lamb (baby sheep). We are not going to wrap our meat in banana leaves, either, and because most of us don't have access to a traditional in-ground Mayan oven called a *pib* (aka our next backyard project), we'll braise ours in a boring old home oven.

The hominy component is a real wild card, too. It's not typical of this Yucatán dish *at all,* but it adds great texture and a bit of brightness. Now that we think about it, the only thing that's really *cochinita pibil*-y about this recipe is the citrus and achiote. But many thanks and a huge shout-out to the people and food culture of the Yucatán for inspiring it.

Serve this dish family-style and let everyone make up their own tacos or bowls.

HOT TIP ★ IF LAMB AIN'T YOUR THING, SUB IN A 3-POUND BONELESS PORK SHOULDER INSTEAD.

Juice of 6 limes
Juice of 2 oranges
1 tablespoon kosher salt
⅓ cup achiote paste
2 heads garlic, halved horizontally
8 sprigs fresh oregano
3 bay leaves

3 pounds boneless lamb shoulder, cut into 2-inch cubes
1 (25-ounce) can hominy, drained and rinsed

FOR SERVING

Pickled red onions, store-bought or homemade (page 113)
Lime wedges
Chopped cilantro
Crumbled Cotija cheese
Corn tortillas or cooked rice

1. In a large Dutch oven, stir together the lime juice, orange juice, salt, and achiote. Add the garlic, oregano, bay leaves, and lamb and stir until coated. Cover the Dutch oven and marinate in the refrigerator for at least 6 hours or up to overnight, stirring occasionally.

2. Preheat the oven to 300°F.

3. Stir the hominy into the Dutch oven, cover, transfer to the oven, and cook until the lamb is tender and easy to pull apart, 3 to 4 hours.

4. Let cool for 15 minutes, then use a slotted spoon to transfer the lamb, garlic, and hominy to a bowl. Discard the oregano and bay leaves. When the garlic heads are cool enough to handle, squeeze them into the bowl and evenly coat the lamb with the garlic, shredding and breaking up the lamb as you go. Skim the fat off the liquid remaining in the Dutch oven and spoon the liquid over the lamb. Season with salt as needed.

5. Serve with the pickled onions, lime wedges, cilantro, Cotija, and tortillas or rice.

SEVEN OF WANDS
PUSHING LIMITS

You're capable of more than you think—even if you think you're capable of a lot. Seek out opportunities to stretch beyond your limits. Start with low-stakes risks to prove to the Universe you're ready to be presented with bigger challenges. Hike the tougher trail. Make your case to get a raise. Sing THAT song at karaoke. Then, speaking of stakes . . . go home and cook yourself this steak. You've earned it.

   The butter in this recipe carries secret magickal agents. Horseradish and leek purify any last drops of doubt within and fill you with courage and vitality. How great is that? All those lessons you worked so hard for, integrating into your body while you recharge.

MAGICKAL INGREDIENTS: HORSERADISH, LEEK (SEE ALLIUMS), BLACK PEPPER

SKIRT STEAK
WITH HORSERADISH-LEEK BUTTER

MAIN —— SERVES 2

The only ingredients here besides the skirt steak are leeks, butter, and horseradish (salt and pepper don't count, silly), so the quality of the steak itself has the power to make or break this dish. Please buy yours from a reputable butcher (actually, you should always do this, not just for this recipe).

   The most important part is to get a good char on one side, because that's where all the flavor lives. (The flavor does not actually live in Flavortown, as a certain delightful chef might have you believe.) Keep it simple by serving it next to some roasted potatoes and a bowl of greens lightly dressed with olive oil and lemon juice.

HOT TIP ★ SKIRT STEAK IS BEST COOKED TO RARE OR MEDIUM-RARE, OTHERWISE IT TENDS TO GET TOUGH.

1 pound skirt steak
Kosher salt and freshly ground black pepper
4 tablespoons (2 ounces) unsalted butter
1 small leek, white part only, finely chopped
About 1 tablespoon prepared horseradish
2 tablespoons grapeseed or canola oil

1. **PREPARE THE STEAK:** Season the steak liberally with salt and pepper and refrigerate for at least 2 and up to 4 hours.

2. Place 2 tablespoons of the butter in a heatproof medium bowl and set aside.

3. In a medium skillet, melt the remaining 2 tablespoons butter over medium-low heat. Add the leek and season with salt. Partially cover the skillet and cook, stirring occasionally, until soft, about 10 minutes.

4. Immediately pour the hot butter and cooked leeks into the bowl with the reserved butter and stir to combine, until all the room temperature butter has melted. Add the horseradish to taste by stirring in up to 1 tablespoon, 1 teaspoon at a time. Let the mixture cool to room temperature, stirring occasionally, until it solidifies, but is still quite soft.

5. Meanwhile, pat the steaks dry. In a large cast-iron skillet or grill pan, heat the oil over high heat. When the oil shimmers, add the steaks and sear until charred, about 4 minutes. Flip, and cook 3 to 4 minutes longer for medium-rare.

6. Transfer to a cutting board, top with the horseradish-leek butter, and let rest for 10 minutes. Slice the steak against the grain to serve.

EIGHT OF WANDS
FINDING YOUR STRIDE

Start planning ahead. The pace you set for yourself now will stick around for a while, so make sure it's sustainable. Make long-term goals and do something to pull them closer every day, even if it's simply thanking the Universe for helping. This does not mean you should settle into a routine—quite the opposite. Always be on the lookout for creative solutions and be ready to adjust the plan if circumstances change.

The marinade for these lamb chops is full of magickal ingredients. Cumin for dedication to stay true to your pace, turmeric for good luck and pure intentions, lemon to cleanse any energies holding you back, and a few others you can read about in the Magickal Ingredient Pantry (page 12).

MAGICKAL INGREDIENTS: CUMIN, TURMERIC, MINT, CILANTRO, LEMON, CAYENNE, PAPRIKA, GARLIC (SEE ALLIUMS), SERRANO PEPPER (SEE CHILES), SHALLOT (SEE ALLIUMS)

LAMB POPS
WITH MINT SALSA VERDE

MAIN —— SERVES 2

A note from Courtney: I learned this simple way of cooking lamb chops from a wonderful Southern Indian woman—the mother of a dear friend of mine. The salsa verde is a little addition I made up for the end, but I think she'd be okay with serving it this way. Oh, and be sure to use the thinner "European-style" yogurt, not Greek.

LAMB

½ cup whole-milk plain yogurt
2 tablespoons fresh lemon juice
1 teaspoon ground coriander
1 teaspoon ground cumin
1 teaspoon garam masala
1 teaspoon hot paprika
1 teaspoon kosher salt
½ teaspoon cayenne pepper
½ teaspoon ground turmeric
3 garlic cloves, minced
6 lamb rib chops, about 1 inch thick

SALSA VERDE

¼ cup extra-virgin olive oil
2 tablespoons finely chopped shallot
1 small serrano pepper, finely chopped
2 tablespoons chopped fresh mint leaves
2 tablespoons chopped fresh cilantro or Italian parsley
2 tablespoons fresh lemon juice
¼ teaspoon kosher salt

TO FINISH

Kosher salt
3 tablespoons extra-virgin olive oil

1. **MARINATE THE LAMB:** In a medium bowl, combine the yogurt, lemon juice, coriander, cumin, garam masala, paprika, salt, cayenne, turmeric, and garlic.

2. Use a paring knife to poke holes in the lamb chops, then put them in a 1-gallon zip-top bag. Add half of the yogurt mixture to the lamb. Using your hands, rub the yogurt all over the lamb, pressing it into the holes. Seal the bag and place in the fridge to marinate for at least 6 hours and up to overnight. Refrigerate the remaining yogurt mixture.

3. **MEANWHILE, MAKE THE SALSA:** In a medium bowl, combine the olive oil, shallot, serrano, mint, cilantro, lemon juice, and salt. Cover the bowl with plastic wrap and chill in the fridge.

4. **TO FINISH:** Remove the lamb chops from the fridge, wipe off any excess yogurt (they should not be completely clean), and season them with salt.

5. In a large skillet, heat the olive oil over medium-high heat. When it shimmers, add the chops and sear, without moving them, until they are browned and crisp, about 4 minutes. Flip and cook about 4 more minutes to medium-rare. Using tongs, flip the chops onto their edges and sear for 1 minute each.

HOT TIP ★ IF YOUR CHOPS ARE THICKER THAN 1½ INCHES, YOU'LL NEED TO COOK THEM UP TO 6 MINUTES PER SIDE FOR MEDIUM-RARE. IF THEY ARE THINNER, COOK ABOUT 3 MINUTES PER SIDE FOR MEDIUM-RARE.

6. Spoon the salsa over the chops and serve with the remaining yogurt on the side.

NINE OF WANDS
RECOGNIZING MASTERY

The best skills are the ones we can spend a lifetime developing and still know we have more to learn. Knowing what you *don't* know is the key to being truly great at something. Identify exactly what skill you want to master and prioritize it. You're stepping into energy that will attract others you can both learn from and offer guidance to. Put it to good use.

An example of not putting it to good use? Trying to improve on perfection. That's wasted energy. Enjoy the perfection, don't seek to alter it. Practice this delicate balance with these crispy ground beef and pickle tacos. The cayenne will keep you passionate about your goals while the garlic shakes out anything in the way.

MAGICKAL INGREDIENTS: CAYENNE PEPPER, GARLIC (SEE ALLIUMS), CHILES, CUMIN, ONION (SEE ALLIUMS)

CRISPY GROUND BEEF AND PICKLE TACOS

MAIN —— SERVES 4

This particular taco is in honor of Malo in the Los Feliz neighborhood of Los Angeles. Unfortunately, Malo has shuttered, but we went there regularly to sit on the back patio, drink margaritas, and talk shop. We came up with the idea for *Divine Your Dinner* over a platter of these very tacos. It seems like a strange combination until you think about it . . . then it seems like the *perfect* combination. Ground beef and pickles with a crunchy exterior? DUH.

You don't have to deep-fry the taco shells ahead of time. You fry them up with the meat already inside in a shallow amount of oil and flip them halfway through cooking. This process leaves the folded seam of the shell slightly soft so you can easily pry open the taco and fill it up with the cheese and pickles. Serve them family-style with the rest of the fixings on the side and let eaters assemble their tacos however they like.

2 tablespoons extra-virgin olive oil

2 tablespoons chili powder

1 tablespoon ground cumin

1 tablespoon garlic powder

1 teaspoon cayenne pepper

1 large yellow onion, finely chopped

3 serrano peppers, seeded and finely chopped

Kosher salt

6 garlic cloves, chopped

1 pound lean ground beef

1 small bunch cilantro stems, finely chopped

1 lime, halved

12 (6-inch) corn tortillas

¼ cup canola or vegetable oil, plus more for brushing the tortillas

FOR SERVING

1 cup shredded cheddar cheese

About 1 cup drained dill pickle chips, store-bought or homemade (page 113)

Salsa, of your choosing

Sour cream

Chopped iceberg lettuce

1. In a 12-inch nonstick skillet, heat the oil over low heat. When it just starts to shimmer, add the chili powder, cumin, garlic powder, and cayenne and toast until fragrant, about 2 minutes.

2. Stir in the onion and serranos, increase the heat to medium, and sauté until the onions are just starting to soften and become translucent, about 5 minutes. Season with salt, add the garlic, and cook 2 minutes more. Add the beef and cook, breaking it up often with a wooden spoon, until browned with a very fine texture, about 15 minutes. Season with salt to taste.

3. Reduce the heat to medium-low, add ½ cup water to the pan, and scrape the browned bits from the bottom. Stir in the cilantro stems and add the lime, cut-sides down. Simmer until most of the water has evaporated, about 10 minutes. Transfer the mixture to a medium bowl and let it cool for 15 minutes. Squeeze the lime juice into the mixture (discard the spent limes).

4. Wipe out the skillet and preheat the oven to 400°F.

5. Using a pastry brush or your fingers, brush both sides of each tortilla with some oil. Lay them in a single layer on a baking sheet (it's okay if they overlap) and bake them until soft and pliable, but not browned, about 4 minutes. Remove them from the oven and set aside.

6. Reduce the oven temperature to 200°F. Line a sheet pan with paper towels.

7. Fill each tortilla with 2 heaping tablespoons of the beef mixture and fold them in half around the filling.

HOT TIP ★ IF THE TACO DOESN'T STAY CLOSED ON ITS OWN, USE A TOOTHPICK TO HOLD THE TWO EDGES TOGETHER.

8. In the same skillet, heat the ¼ cup oil over medium-high heat. When it shimmers, arrange 4 tacos at a time in the skillet and fry until browned, about 3 minutes per side, adjusting the temperature as necessary so they fry in the 3-minute timeframe.

9. Transfer the tacos to the lined sheet pan and keep them warm in the oven while you fry the rest.

10. To serve, stuff each taco with cheddar and pickle chips. Serve with the salsa, sour cream, and chopped lettuce on the side.

TEN OF WANDS
INTEGRATING VITALITY

This level of your creative adventure is complete. You have reached the apex of development, becoming good friends with your inner voice, unafraid to take risks, creative and playful in the formation of your life. Enjoy it. And while you do, look out for where you're being pulled next. To keep on growing, you'll have to bring your skills to a new challenge after you complete your work here.

This giant sandwich is not for the faint of heart. It is the pinnacle of sandwich creation and will impart knowledge and skills you can use in future kitchen pursuits. Bay leaves and thyme leave you braver and a little more psychic than you were before.

MAGICKAL INGREDIENTS: BAY LEAVES, THYME, OREGANO, GARLIC (SEE ALLIUMS), ONION (SEE ALLIUMS), BLACK PEPPER, JALAPEÑO (SEE CHILES)

GIANT ROAST PORK SANDWICHES

MAIN —— SERVES 3 TO 4

Don't skip this recipe. If you have to, you can make half of it and assemble one sandwich instead of two. But please don't skip it. It's decadent. It's juicy. It's . . . dare we say . . . ONE OF THE GREATEST SANDWICHES OF ALL TIME!!!

The recipe makes about 2 cups more pork than you'll need, but it freezes well, and you can use it for tacos, in ragu for pasta, as a filling for dumplings, or you can eat it plain with a spoon.

The mayonnaise measurements make the perfect amount to assemble this sandwich, with no leftovers, but, like the sandwich it's used in, this mayo is one of the GREATEST MAYOS OF ALL TIME (G.M.O.A.T.), so consider doubling or tripling it so you have some for a rainy day. It'll last up to a month in your fridge.

PULLED PORK

3 pound boneless pork butt

Kosher salt and freshly ground black pepper

1 head garlic, halved horizontally

2 medium yellow onions, roughly chopped

8 sprigs fresh oregano

12 sprigs fresh thyme

4 bay leaves

4 cups chicken broth, store-bought or homemade (page 32)

G.M.O.A.T. (MAYONNAISE)

1 cup mayonnaise

6 garlic cloves, minced

½ cup finely chopped pepperoncini or pickled jalapeños

2 tablespoons pepperoncini or pickled jalapeño juice

SANDWICHES

3 tablespoons canola or peanut oil

6 medium shallots, cut into ¼-inch-thick rounds

Kosher salt

2 French bread loaves (14 inches long)

10 ounces P'tit Basque or Gruyère cheese, rind removed and thinly sliced

1. Preheat the oven to 300°F.

2. **MAKE THE PULLED PORK:** Season the pork all over with salt and pepper. Place the pork in a 9 × 13-inch roasting pan and add the garlic, onions, oregano, thyme, bay leaves, and chicken broth. Transfer to the oven and cook, basting occasionally, until browned, about 4 hours. Cover with foil and cook until tender and falling apart, 2 to 3 hours longer.

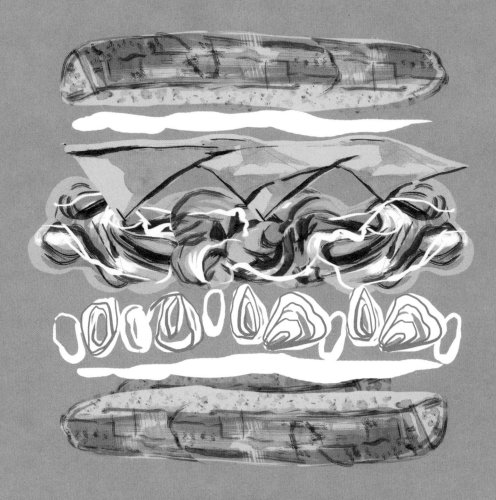

3. **MEANWHILE, MAKE THE G.M.O.A.T. (MAYONNAISE):** In a small bowl, combine the mayonnaise, garlic, pepperoncini, and pepperoncini juice. Cover and refrigerate to chill.

4. **FOR THE SANDWICHES:** In a large skillet, heat the oil over high heat until the oil shimmers. Working in 2 or 3 batches (do not overcrowd the pan), add the shallots in a single layer. Cook without stirring until very dark brown, about 4 minutes per batch. Remove the shallots from the skillet, season them with salt, and let cool.

5. Remove the pork from the oven. Leave the oven on and increase the oven temperature to 350°F.

6. Let the pork cool slightly. Discard the herb sprigs and bay leaves and squeeze the garlic out of the skin into the pan. Use a potato masher or the back of a spoon to mash the garlic and onions into a chunky paste in the liquid. Using two forks, shred the pork, combine with the juices, and season with salt and pepper to taste.

7. Split each baguette in half lengthwise and scoop out a little bit of the bread to make room for all the toppings.

8. To assemble the sandwiches, lay two double layers of foil on a flat work surface. Place the bottom half of each baguette on a piece of foil and spread ¼ cup of the G.M.O.A.T. on each piece. Dividing evenly, layer the cheese on top of the mayonnaise. Add a healthy layer of pulled pork to each loaf, then top with the shallots. Spread ¼ cup mayonnaise on each of the remaining baguette halves and place atop the bottom halves. Press down to flatten. Wrap each sandwich in the foil, place on a sheet pan, and bake until the cheese has melted, about 15 minutes.

9. Cut each sandwich into thirds or halves to serve.

PAGE OF WANDS

EARTH OF FIRE ★ EXPLORING CREATIVITY

Just because it's familiar doesn't mean it's ideal. Get out of your routine and find new, more enjoyable and efficient ways to accomplish both mundane and fantastical tasks. Stretch your abilities, revisit abandoned techniques, play. Give yourself the gift of being bad at something. Nothing opens up hidden talents faster than failing and needing to improvise.

New skills offer new means of expression, so if you find yourself suddenly needing to let it all out on the dance floor, just go with it. Get wild, do things you normally wouldn't do—like putting all your bananas in one basket, as we've done with this dessert. The vanilla will have you teaming up with the unexplored part of yourself most likely to lead you into new territory.

MAGICKAL INGREDIENTS: BANANA, VANILLA

BANANAS FOSTER PUDDING CUPS

DESSERT —— SERVES 6

This is a mash-up of two excellent bananacentric desserts: banana pudding and bananas Foster. Because why have one when you can have both? Plus, if a flambé doesn't go along perfectly with a Fire element tarot card, then we don't know what does.

Make sure everyone is watching when you flambé the bananas because it's *real* impressive. But if for some reason yours don't ignite, it's totally okay. Just continue cooking the sauce for a minute to cook the alcohol off before serving.

LITERAL HOT TIP ★ WE DO NOT CONDONE ACCIDENTALLY SETTING YOUR KITCHEN ON FIRE. FLAMBÉ CAREFULLY AND AT YOUR OWN RISK.

PUDDING

¾ cup granulated sugar

¼ cup cornstarch

¼ teaspoon kosher salt

4 large egg yolks

4 cups whole milk

1 teaspoon pure vanilla extract

2 tablespoons unsalted butter

¼ cup canned sweetened condensed milk

1 (11-ounce) box vanilla wafer cookies, such as Nilla wafers

BANANAS

3 tablespoons unsalted butter

2 tablespoons light brown sugar

3 large ripe bananas, cut into ¼-inch rounds

6 tablespoons 80- to 90-proof spiced rum

1. **MAKE THE PUDDING:** In a large saucepan, whisk together the granulated sugar, cornstarch, and salt. Whisk in the egg yolks and milk, then cook over medium-high heat, whisking often, until it begins to bubble in the middle and around the edges. Reduce the heat to medium and cook 30 seconds longer, whisking constantly.

2. Remove the pan from the heat and whisk in the vanilla, butter, and condensed milk. Pour the mixture into a large, shallow dish, cover with plastic wrap so it touches the mixture, and refrigerate for at least 4 hours to set.

3. Add the wafers to a large zip-top bag and crush them with your hands until chunky. Add a thin layer of crushed wafers to the bottoms of six 8-ounce glasses or bowls. Add ¼ cup of pudding to each glass. Smooth the pudding out with a spoon and sprinkle a thin layer of wafers on top. Divide the remaining pudding evenly among the glasses and finish with another layer of wafer crumbles. Loosely cover the pudding cups with plastic wrap and refrigerate for at least 4 hours or up to overnight.

4. **FOR THE PIÈCE DE RÉSISTANCE, MAKE THE BANANAS:** In a medium skillet, melt the butter and brown sugar over medium heat. Add the bananas and cook, stirring occasionally, until they start to caramelize, about 7 minutes. Remove the skillet from heat, add the rum, and ignite it using a long stick lighter. Swirl the sauce around until the flame is extinguished.

5. Divide the flambéed bananas evenly among the 6 cups and serve immediately.

KNIGHT OF WANDS

FIRE OF FIRE ★ RACING TO ACTION

Your restless fidgeting is growing into full-fledged pacing. All that energy is gonna go somewhere and it's up to you to direct it. Sift through the intensity to find what's fueling it. These times don't come around often and when they do, you want to make sure you use your power to revitalize a goal or cause you are passionate about. Fortunately, all this Fire energy means it should be easy to hear your guiding intuition.

Let off some of the steam clouding your mind by lighting actual fires on top of this mai tai tiki party cake. The pineapple brings luck to ensure you're going to run in the right direction and lime protects you from being burned . . . metaphorically. Taking care to not get physically burned is on you.

MAGICKAL INGREDIENTS: PINEAPPLE, LIME, VANILLA

FLAMING MAI TAI TIKI PARTY CAKE

DESSERT —— SERVES 20

A note from Courtney: On top of bringing food and tarot together for a magickal eating experience, the secret, secondary goal of this cookbook (that I'm not sure Melinda is aware of) is for me to bring back the art of flambéed desserts. These desserts had their heyday back in mid-century times, but the Bananas Foster Pudding Cups (page 75), Baked Alaska with Cinnamon Toast Crumbs (page 52), and Crepes SUZE-ette (page 78) are merely the tip of the iceberg. This cake is the rest of the iceberg. The part you didn't see coming. Yes, this recipe is a lot of work, but it's worth it, plus you get to drink mai tais along the way, so it feels like a vacation.

To present the cake, you'll decorate it with hollowed-out limes that are filled with 151-proof rum and set them ablaze like a flaming tiki drink. At this point, you'll need to be extra careful because you will be a walking fire hazard and probably a little tipsy from all those mai tais you drank earlier, but dammit if this isn't the best cake presentation of all time.

HOT TIP ★ THE RECIPE CALLS FOR 4 LIME HALVES TO DECORATE THE CAKE WITH AND SET ABLAZE, BUT YOU COULD USE AS MANY AS YOU WANT—COVER THE ENTIRE THING AND GO FOR FULL-ON BONFIRE VIBES. OR, IF YOU ARE CONCERNED ABOUT SAFETY, OMIT THE FLAMING LIMES ALTOGETHER AND SET ASIDE SOME OF THE CARAMELIZED PINEAPPLE TO DECORATE THE TOP OF YOUR CAKE INSTEAD.

CAKE

2½ cups all-purpose flour

1¼ teaspoons baking powder

1¼ teaspoons kosher salt

2 sticks (8 ounces) unsalted butter, at room temperature

1¾ cups granulated sugar

½ cup packed light brown sugar

4 large eggs

4 large egg yolks

½ cup grapeseed oil

2 teaspoons pure vanilla extract

1 cup plus 2 tablespoons whole milk

MAI TAI SOAK

1½ sticks (6 ounces) unsalted butter

¾ cup granulated sugar

½ cup spiced rum

Juice of 2 limes

3 tablespoons Curaçao

4½ teaspoons orgeat syrup

CARAMELIZED PINEAPPLE

1 pineapple, peeled, cored, and cut into ½-inch chunks

2 tablespoons light brown sugar

¼ teaspoon kosher salt

LIME FROSTING

4 sticks (16 ounces) unsalted butter, at room temperature

2⅔ cups powdered sugar

Grated zest of 4 limes

3 tablespoons freshly squeezed lime juice

⅓ teaspoon kosher salt

FOR PRESENTATION (OPTIONAL)

2 limes, halved

2 teaspoons 151-proof rum

1. Preheat the oven to 350°F and position the rack so it's in the center of the oven. Grease two 9 × 13-inch sheet pans and line with parchment paper so the parchment paper sticks to the pans.

2. **MAKE THE CAKE:** In a medium bowl, combine the flour, baking powder, and salt.

3. In a stand mixer fitted with the paddle, cream the butter, granulated sugar, and brown sugar on medium-high speed until light and fluffy, about 3 minutes. Scrape down the sides of the bowl with a spatula.

4. With the mixer on low, add the whole eggs and egg yolks one at a time, letting each addition incorporate fully before adding another. Slowly pour in the grapeseed oil and vanilla, increase the speed to high, and whip for 3 minutes, until light and fluffy. Scrape down the sides of the bowl with a spatula.

5. Reduce the speed to low and add the flour mixture in three additions, alternating with the milk, beginning and ending with the flour. Mix until just combined. Scrape down the sides of the bowl with a spatula, then divide the batter between the two lined sheet pans.

6. Bake the cakes until they begin pulling away from the sides of the pan and bounce back when you lightly tap the top, about 30 minutes, rotating them front to back halfway through.

7. **MEANWHILE, MAKE THE MAI TAI SOAK:** In a medium saucepan, combine the butter, granulated sugar, spiced rum, lime juice, Curaçao, and orgeat and bring to a simmer over low heat until the butter has melted and the sugar has dissolved. Remove from the heat and set aside until the cakes are done baking.

HOT TIP ★ WHILE YOU'RE WAITING, MAKE YOURSELF A MAI TAI (YOU DO ALREADY HAVE ALL THE INGREDIENTS ON HAND AND YOU DESERVE IT).

8. Remove the cakes from the oven but leave the oven on and increase the oven temperature to 450°F (for the caramelized pineapple).

9. Use a paring knife to poke holes all over the cakes. While the cakes are still hot, pour the mai tai soak evenly over both cakes. Let the cakes cool to room temperature, then wrap them tightly and store them in the fridge until you are ready to assemble them.

10. **MAKE THE CARAMELIZED PINEAPPLE:** In a sheet pan, combine the pineapple chunks, brown sugar, and salt and toss to coat. Bake, stirring occasionally, until dark and caramelized, about 30 minutes.

11. **MEANWHILE, MAKE THE LIME FROSTING:** In a stand mixer fitted with the paddle, cream the butter on high for about 3 minutes, until smooth. Scrape down the sides of the bowl and add the powdered sugar, lime zest, and salt. Mix on low until the powdered sugar is incorporated, then increase the speed to high and mix 3 more minutes, until the frosting is light and fluffy and has doubled in size. Reduce the speed to low and gradually add the lime juice. Increase the speed to high and beat 1 minute more.

12. Run a knife around the edges of both sheet pans and invert one of the cakes onto a clean sheet of parchment paper. Remove the used parchment paper from the bottom of the cake and return the cake and clean parchment to the pan, bottom-side up. Using a spoon or an offset spatula, spread one-quarter of the lime frosting evenly over the top of the cake. Add the pineapple in an even layer, then spread another one-quarter of the lime frosting on top of the pineapple. Invert the second cake on top of the first one. Press down slightly, then remove the used parchment and spread the remaining lime frosting evenly over the top. Style the frosting with swoops and swirls or make it smooth.

13. Refrigerate the cake for 1 hour to chill, then wrap it loosely with plastic wrap and refrigerate until you are ready to present it. The cake will keep in the fridge for up to 4 days or in the freezer for up to 1 month.

14. To serve, unwrap the cake and let it sit at room temperature for 1 hour. If presenting the cake with the flaming lime halves, scoop out the meat of the 4 lime halves and place on top of the cake, cut-side up. Fill each with ½ teaspoon of the 151-proof rum and light them on fire.

There is a line in the sand and you've crossed it. You can no longer pretend to be enthusiastic about things you don't truly care for. Your energy must be spent working *with* your heart. This doesn't mean you have to absolutely love every task of your day, but they should all be related to supporting personal goals.

Whatever it is you're moving toward, your heartfelt passion makes you well positioned to inspire others to join you. Lure them in further with these crepes SUZE-ette. The magickal properties of sweet citrus will lift everyone's mood, leaving the whole lot eager to join the cause. And if that doesn't work, the Suze will.

MAGICKAL INGREDIENT: MANDARIN ORANGE (SEE ORANGE)

CREPES SUZE-ETTE

DESSERT —— SERVES 4 TO 6

Suze is a neon yellow liqueur that's made from gentian root. It's bitter, bright, citrusy, and a boon to any liquor cabinet. Here we add it to the sauce that the crepes are cooked in for a twist on a traditional crepes suzette. However, if you don't want to buy a whole bottle of Suze just for this recipe, you can substitute brandy. (But we really do hope you get the Suze.)

The sauce calls for fresh mandarin orange juice—use that if you can. The juice is extra sweet and balances the bitterness of the Suze. However, you can use any other type of sweet orange juice as well. Cara Cara, tangerine, or even blood orange will do the trick.

When you make the crepes, it will probably take a few times to get right. The recipe makes about 16 crepes, which is more than you will need, so if you have a few fallen soldiers, no big deal.

HOT TIP ★ MAKE SURE EVERYONE IS WATCHING WHEN YOU FLAMBÉ THE CREPES BECAUSE IT'S *REAL* IMPRESSIVE. BUT IF FOR SOME REASON YOURS DOESN'T IGNITE, IT'S TOTALLY OKAY. CONTINUE COOKING THE SAUCE FOR A MINUTE TO COOK THE ALCOHOL OFF AND SERVE.

CREPES

1½ cups whole milk

1½ cups all-purpose flour

3 large eggs

3 tablespoons sugar

4 tablespoons (2 ounces) unsalted butter, melted and cooled to room temperature

½ teaspoon kosher salt

FOR THE SUZE-ETTE

1 stick (4 ounces) unsalted butter

2 teaspoons grated orange zest

1 cup freshly squeezed mandarin orange juice

½ cup sugar

3 tablespoons Suze liqueur or brandy

1. MAKE THE CREPES: In a blender, combine the milk, flour, eggs, sugar, melted butter, and salt and blend until a smooth batter forms. Let the batter sit for 15 minutes.

2. Mist a nonstick medium skillet with cooking spray and heat over medium heat. Using a ¼-cup dry measure, add 1 scant scoop of batter to the skillet. Tilt the pan in all directions to swirl the batter around until the bottom of the skillet is evenly coated. When bubbles start to form on the surface, flip with a spatula and cook 30 seconds more until golden brown.

HOT TIP ★ IF THE BATTER IS TOO THICK TO SPREAD, ADD UP TO 4 TABLESPOONS OF WATER, ONE AT A TIME.

3. Stack the cooked crepes on a plate as you work and repeat with the remaining batter, remisting the skillet after every 3 crepes. Take as few as 8 or as many as 12 crepes and fold them into quarters, first by folding them in half, them folding them again into a triangle shape.

4. MAKE THE SUZE-ETTE: In a separate 12-inch skillet, combine the butter, orange zest, orange juice, and sugar over medium-high heat. Bring the mixture to a simmer and cook, stirring often, until the mixture reduces to a syrup, 7 to 10 minutes.

5. Turn the heat off and arrange the folded crepes on top of the sauce along the edge of the pan in a circular pattern, overlapping slightly. To do so, use tongs to first dip one side of the folded crepe in the sauce, then flip it over and place the crepe in the pan with the undipped side down. This way both sides of the crepe get covered in the sauce.

Return the pan to medium-high heat and cook until the syrup starts to bubble, then reduce the heat to low and cook until the crepes are warmed through, about 5 minutes.

6. Transfer the crepes to a platter. Return the skillet to the heat and bring the syrup back to a boil. Add the Suze to the pan, turn off the heat, and ignite the syrup with a long stick lighter. Swirl the syrup around until the flame extinguishes, pour it over the crepes, and serve immediately.

KING OF WANDS

All words are magick words. Our statements are incantations, reverberating through the Universe, affecting change, great and small. You have a lot to say right now and you possess the strategic vision to speak your mind when and how it will be most powerful. Be mindful of language you use casually. If you play your cards right, you could make big changes just by speaking them out loud.

    With this much at stake, you want to connect with your whole being. Cocoa opens the heart, allowing your plans to be emotionally and intellectually sound. Cinnamon amplifies self-mastery and magickal ability, and chile bumps up creativity and vitality. All are present in these brownies. Say the magick words and bring them to life. Also, follow the recipe.

MAGICKAL INGREDIENTS: COCOA, CINNAMON, ANCHO CHILE
POWDER (SEE CHILES), VANILLA, PECANS

ANCHO CHILE BROWNIES

DESSERT —— MAKES AN 8-INCH SQUARE PAN

If you are looking for an incredibly simple recipe that yields dense, gooey, fudgy brownies with just a hint of depth, then you have come to the right place. Some people like nuts in their brownies; if you are one of those people, add them. Pecans or walnuts work best, but hazelnuts or slivered almonds would be great, too.

1 stick (4 ounces) unsalted butter, melted

1 cup sugar

⅓ cup Dutch process cocoa powder

2 large eggs

1 teaspoon pure vanilla extract

⅓ cup all-purpose flour

1½ teaspoons ancho chile powder

¾ teaspoon ground cinnamon

½ teaspoon kosher salt

1 cup chopped toasted pecans or walnuts (optional)

1. Preheat the oven to 325°F. Grease an 8 × 8-inch baking dish.

2. In a large bowl, stir together the melted butter, sugar, and cocoa to combine. Whisk in the eggs and vanilla.

3. In a separate large bowl, combine the flour, ancho powder, cinnamon, and salt. Add the flour mixture to the chocolate mixture and mix until just combined. Stir in the nuts (if using).

4. Pour the batter into the prepared dish and bake until the edges are crisp and the center is set, but still a little gooey, about 35 minutes.

5. Let cool completely before slicing.

CUPS

WATER ★ SEAFOOD

THE SEA OF EMOTION

The elemental energy of Water can lift you up or pull you down, cleanse you or drag you through the mud. We need it to survive, but too much can break us apart—from each other and from ourselves, tearing us away from our own battered hearts. Water is probably the easiest element to understand because it behaves so much like the realm it rules: emotion. And though some emotional experiences are definitely more pleasant than others, they are all valuable. We would never know that pure joy was special if we never experienced sadness.

So, let's raise a glass to the Cups! We'll cruise through a variety of preparations of crustaceans, mollusks, and fishes, enjoying the bounty of the sea as manifestations of the ten numbered cards. Then, the court of Neptune sails in, bringing desserts designed to sweeten the mood. Grab your handkerchief and a rose quartz and steady yourself. It could get choppy out there.

ACE OF CUPS
ACCEPTING THE GIFT OF WATER

Memories come flooding back, but not in visual form. Your body feels light and buoyant, then so heavy you can barely lift your arms as emotional memories rush through, leaving bleary vignettes in their wake. Fleeting moments carry huge impact while vast stretches of time barely register. Don't fight it. You are processing a backlog of emotional experiences, being cleansed of their impact, but not of their lessons. Those are yours to keep.

This shellfish broth is a great metaphor for this process. While the creatures are gone and eaten, their shells remain, still having plenty to offer despite being emptied of their previous life. Just go with it. Eat the lessons. They're versatile and extremely enjoyable.

MAGICKAL INGREDIENTS: ONION (SEE ALLIUMS), LEMON, BAY LEAF

SHELLFISH STOCK

BACK POCKET BASIC —— MAKES ABOUT 4 CUPS

About 8 cups shellfish shells
1 large yellow or white onion, quartered
1 lemon, quartered
1 bay leaf

Use this as a base for bisques, chowders, paellas, bouillabaisses, sauces, or any dish that you'd like to add the subtle taste of shellfish to. Similar to vegetable stock (see page 108), you'll collect the shells whenever you make shrimp, crab, crawfish, or lobster, and keep them in the freezer in a bag until you have enough to make a stock.

Take this as a guide more than a recipe. If you end up with tons of shells, go ahead and use them all, they will only make the stock more flavorful. If you have some white wine on hand that you don't want to drink (why?!?), add a splash to the stock. Don't love bay leaves but can't get enough sage in your life? Switch them out!

1. Add the shells to a large stockpot along with the onion, lemon, and bay leaf and add water to cover them by about 2 inches. Cover the pot and bring to a simmer over medium-high heat. Reduce the heat to low and cook for about 1 hour, until fragrant and slightly reduced.

2. Strain the stock through a fine-mesh sieve and discard the solids. Store in an airtight container in the fridge for up to 1 week or in the freezer for 3 months.

TWO OF CUPS

Love isn't truly love until it's shared. The send/receive loop is the circuit that allows the current to spark. To make this possible, you've got to open yourself up to sending and receiving. So, open on up! Showing yourself love is a great way to practice receiving it. Cooking yourself a magickal meal, for example . . .

This one has what it takes to get you completing the love circuit in no time. The bonding influence of lemon is made safe by the protective quality of garlic. Parsley gets you chatting while paprika encourages creativity in how you make your connections. And we'd be remiss if we didn't include a little cayenne for passion. So, we did. You're welcome.

MAGICKAL INGREDIENTS: LEMON, PARSLEY, PAPRIKA, GARLIC (SEE ALLIUMS), CAYENNE, SCALLION (SEE ALLIUMS), BLACK PEPPER, MUSTARD

PAN-FRIED COD
WITH SPICY RÉMOULADE

MAIN —— SERVES 2

A note from Courtney: I had many loves growing up. One of them was Jordan Catalano, and another was the fried cod smothered in tartar sauce from Luby's Cafeteria, a Texas comfort food paradise. Allow me to paint a quick picture: You walk in, get in line (there is *always* a line), and snag a tray. You place it on the rail and start grabbing plates of deliciousness as you slide on down toward the register. There's chicken fried steak, meat loaf, mashed potatoes, mac 'n' cheese, cream gravy, even Jell-O. It's *all* there, but it's the fried cod with tartar sauce that catches your eye. It's perfectly rectangular. It's all you've ever wanted. It's true love.

This recipe is in honor of that dish, but instead of deep-frying it, the cod gets a light dredge in flour before getting pan-fried. If your fishmonger is out of cod, any mild, white, flaky fish—like flounder, sole, trout, or snapper—will work. Cook until it's extra crispy on one side before flipping it over to finish cooking on the other side. And don't be shy with the rémoulade.

RÉMOULADE

¼ cup mayonnaise

2 tablespoons finely chopped dill pickles, store-bought or homemade (see Pickled Veggies, page 113)

2 teaspoons spicy Dijon mustard

1 teaspoon Louisiana-style hot sauce, such as Crystal

1 teaspoon Worcestershire sauce

1 scallion, finely chopped, green part only

1½ teaspoons chopped fresh Italian parsley

¼ teaspoon minced garlic

Pinch cayenne pepper

Kosher salt and freshly ground black pepper

PAN-FRIED COD

2 cod fillets (8 ounces each), about ½ inch thick

Kosher salt and freshly ground black pepper

¼ cup all-purpose flour

3 tablespoons unsalted butter

2 tablespoons extra-virgin olive oil

Lemon wedges, for serving

1. **MAKE THE RÉMOULADE:** In a medium bowl, combine the mayonnaise, pickles, mustard, hot sauce, Worcestershire sauce, scallion, parsley, paprika, and cayenne. Season with salt and black pepper. Cover and refrigerate for at least 1 hour or up to overnight.

2. **PAN-FRY THE COD:** Pat the fish dry and season all over with salt and pepper. Add the flour to a large plate and, working one at a time, dredge each piece of fish in the flour, turning to coat fully.

3. In a large cast-iron skillet, heat the butter and olive oil over medium-high heat. Once the butter has melted, add the fillets, shaking off the excess flour first, and cook until they start to crisp and brown on the edges, 3 to 4 minutes. Flip and cook 2 minutes more.

4. Top with the rémoulade (seriously . . . be *generous*) and serve with lemon wedges.

THREE OF CUPS
FINDING FAMILY

A bond is forming between you and a small group of close friends. You've created a safe zone where you can be loved and accepted for exactly who you are, supported no matter what. These are the shoulders you cry on and the eyes whose tears you dry, the first people you call with important news. This is your chosen family. Treat them like the precious gold they are.

If you need a little jump-start on how to show your fam you love them, may we suggest this lovely shrimp-based snack? It is both delicious and nutritious. And by nutritious, we mean dusted with magick to make sure those bonds keep you as tightly glued to each other as you're going to be to the bowl.

MAGICKAL INGREDIENTS: CILANTRO, GARLIC (SEE ALLIUMS), SCALLION (SEE ALLIUMS), SERRANO PEPPER (SEE CHILES), FRESNO CHILE (SEE CHILES), CELERY, SESAME OIL, CHILI OIL (SEE CHILES), MITSUBA

TIGER SALAD "CEVICHE"

SNACK —— SERVES 2 TO 4

Tiger salad is a Northern Chinese dish also called *lao hu cai*. Somewhere between a salad and a condiment, it usually consists of lots of herbs and chiles chopped together with some vinegar, and is used to brighten any dish. This is a light, crisp, and refreshing take on *lao hu cai* with lots of garlicky, buttery hunks of shrimp added to it. And "ceviche" is in quotes because the shrimp in this recipe is cooked over heat, instead of with acidity, which is how the raw seafood in a traditional ceviche is "cooked."

Serve chilled or at room temperature scooped onto chips or the Rosemary Salt(ines) (page 160). It's perfect for snacking on the couch while basking in the glow of the television.

HOT TIP ★ IF YOU CAN'T FIND MITSUBA, YOU CAN SUBSTITUTE A 1:1 RATIO OF ITALIAN PARSLEY AND CHERVIL. THE DISH WILL STILL BE GREAT, BUT SERIOUSLY, TRY TO FIND MITSUBA IF YOU CAN.

1 tablespoon unsalted butter

1 tablespoon extra-virgin olive oil

½ pound shrimp, peeled and deveined (tails removed)

Kosher salt

2 cloves garlic, minced

½ cup finely diced Persian (mini) cucumber

1 scallion, dark green tops only, finely chopped

1 small serrano pepper, seeded and finely chopped

1 red Fresno chile, seeded and finely chopped

3 tablespoons finely chopped celery

2 tablespoons chopped celery leaves

5 large shiso leaves, chopped

3 tablespoons chopped mitsuba

3 tablespoons chopped fresh cilantro

2 tablespoons rice vinegar

1 tablespoon toasted sesame oil

½ teaspoon sugar

Chili oil (optional), for serving

Tortilla chips or Rosemary Salt(ines) (page 160), for serving

1. In a large nonstick skillet, melt the butter and olive oil over medium-high heat. Season the shrimp all over with salt, then add them to the skillet in one layer and cook on one side until browned on the bottom and slightly opaque, about 2 minutes. Reduce the heat to medium-low, add the garlic, toss, and cook 1 minute more, until completely opaque.

2. Remove the shrimp from the skillet and let cool for 10 minutes. Chop them into ¼-inch pieces, then mix them with the garlicky butter in the skillet. Transfer to a bowl and let cool in the fridge.

3. Meanwhile, in a large bowl, combine the cucumber, scallion greens, serrano, Fresno chile, celery, celery leaves, shiso, mitsuba, cilantro, vinegar, sesame oil, sugar, and ½ teaspoon salt.

4. Add the shrimp and stir to combine. Taste and season with salt as needed. Drizzle some chili oil on top (if using) and serve with tortilla chips or Rosemary Salt(ines) (page 160). Store in an airtight container in the fridge for up to 2 days.

FOUR OF CUPS

SETTING BOUNDARIES

Steady, now. Let the waters within and around you get very still. So still you can see your reflection clearly. And then imagine what you want for that person, how you want them to care and be cared for. You're in a good place to set some emotional boundaries. It's a delicate balance: too strong and you'll isolate yourself, too weak and you'll become exhausted caring for the needs of others while yours go unmet.

Fortunately, the magickal ingredient from that ruler of balance, Justice (see page 153), is here to help. Olives and olive oil form the basis of this poached tuna recipe, infusing the whole enterprise with contentment, stability, and healing. Enjoy it over some mutually respectful conversation with someone you love.

MAGICKAL INGREDIENTS: OLIVES, CAPER BERRIES, MARJORAM, GARLIC (SEE ALLIUMS), LEMON, PARSLEY, POTATOES

POACHED TUNA

WITH ROASTED POTATOES AND OLIVES

MAIN —— SERVES 2

This mash-up of Niçoise salad and potato salad is great as a main dish, but also works as a side. Please note that we use caper *berries,* not capers. Caper berries are a larger, milder version of the tiny caper we all know and love. To elaborate further, capers are the buds of the caper bush and the caper *berries* are what you'll get if you let those buds turn into beautiful flowers, then let the flowers wilt, fall off, and be replaced by the fruits of the caper bush—the berries!

HOT TIP ★ BE SURE TO SAVE THAT LEFTOVER TUNA GARLIC OIL TO MAKE A REALLY GOOD SALAD DRESSING— THE CHICORY CAESAR (PAGE 147), PERHAPS?

½ pound ahi tuna, 1½ inches thick

Kosher salt

1 pound fingerling potatoes

1 cup extra-virgin olive oil

¾ cup pitted green olives

4 caper berries

6 cloves garlic, peeled

Grated zest and juice of 1 lemon

6 sprigs fresh marjoram or oregano

Chopped Italian parsley, for serving

1. Place the tuna in a large shallow bowl and season all over with 2 teaspoons kosher salt. Cover with plastic wrap and let cure in the fridge for 2 hours.

2. Meanwhile, in a large pot, combine the potatoes and water to cover and bring to a boil over medium-high heat. Cook until fork-tender, about 25 minutes. Drain and let cool. Halve the potatoes.

3. In a 1-quart pot, combine the oil, olives, caper berries, garlic, lemon zest, and marjoram and heat over very low heat. Using a potato masher, gently mash the olives, caper berries, and garlic and cook until the garlic becomes soft and browned— about 20 minutes. Remove the pot from the heat and set aside for everything to infuse.

4. In a 10-inch nonstick or cast-iron skillet, heat 3 tablespoons of the garlic-infused oil over medium-high heat. When the oil shimmers, add the potatoes in a single layer, season with salt, and cook them without stirring until they start to brown, about 4 minutes. Stir the potatoes and cook until crispy, about 4 minutes longer. Transfer the potatoes to a large bowl.

5. Discard the marjoram stems and use a slotted spoon to scoop the olives, garlic, and caper berries out of the infused oil and add them to the bowl of potatoes. Cover the bowl with plastic wrap and let cool to room temperature.

6. Heat the infused oil to 200°F (use an instant-read meat thermometer to measure the temp). Rinse the tuna, pat dry, and add to the oil. Poach for 6 to 7 minutes, flipping it halfway through, until barely cooked through. Remove from the heat and let cool in the oil for about 20 minutes.

7. Transfer the tuna to the potato mixture and use a fork to flake it into large chunks. Add the lemon juice and parsley and toss to coat. Taste and add salt as needed. Serve at room temp or slightly warmed.

FIVE OF CUPS
ALLOWING EXPRESSION

Sometimes you gotta let it all out. This is one of those times. Bottling up emotions doesn't make them go away. Sometimes it's been so long, we don't even know what the feeling is attached to anymore. That's okay. You don't have to figure anything out (that's more of a Swords thing anyway). Just give your emotional body permission to express itself.

   With deference to the fabulous pop song by Madonna, we have what we think is a pretty great way to inspire self-expression. These salmon toasts are versatile: great for a night alone, processing a newly released tidal wave, or with friends to witness your emotional emancipation. Dill keeps your mind at an observational distance while radish keeps you and your feelings safe and sound.

MAGICKAL INGREDIENTS: DILL, RADISH, MUSTARD

SMOKY SALMON TOASTS

SNACK —— MAKES 16 TOASTS

Smoked salmon comes two ways: hot or cold. Cold-smoked is similar to lox in that it's not "cooked" but cured with a low-temperature smoking technique. Hot-smoked is cooked in a similar way to BBQ—it's hot, fully cooked through, and generally has a smokier taste than its cold counterpart. For this recipe, use hot-smoked salmon. You can smoke your own or buy any kind you like from most grocery stores.

4 slices rye or pumpernickel bread, crusts removed and cut into 16 triangles

¼ cup crème fraîche

1 tablespoon grainy Dijon mustard

Pinch of kosher salt

4 ounces hot-smoked salmon, crumbled

¼ cup thinly sliced radishes

¼ cup finely diced dill pickles, store-bought or homemade (see Pickled Veggies, page 113)

2 teaspoons chopped fresh dill

1. Preheat the oven to 400°F.

2. Arrange the bread triangles on a baking sheet and toast until they are crusty and browned on the edges, about 7 minutes. Remove from the oven and let cool to room temperature.

3. In a small bowl, combine the crème fraîche, mustard, and salt. Spread the toasts with the crème fraîche mixture, then top with salmon, radishes, pickles, and dill to serve.

SIX OF CUPS
GAINING EXPERIENCE

Take a deep, cleansing breath and pause for a moment. Notice the shift that has happened in your relational life. You no longer react to things that once provoked you. Friends who once counseled you now come to you for guidance. You don't get as attached, yet you love more fiercely. Congratulations! You're building emotional maturity! Continue to grow your empathy and compassion from here.

Start by inviting a friend over for some spicy fish noodles. The powerhouses of this dish are ginger and garlic. Ginger (see Strength, page 148) is a powerful activator of the Fire center, boosting the bravery and sharp instinct needed to open challenging conversations. Garlic is the go-to for clearing and protecting, so you'll be unlikely to have any crossed wires.

MAGICKAL INGREDIENTS: GINGER, GARLIC (SEE ALLIUMS), CILANTRO, SCALLIONS (SEE ALLIUMS), LEMON, SICHUAN PEPPERCORNS, GOCHUGARU (SEE CHILES)

SPICY FISH NOODLES
WITH GINGER AND SCALLIONS

MAIN —— SERVES 2 TO 3

If Sichuan boiled fish and pasta aglio e olio had a baby, it would look something like this. The fish breaks down as you toss it with the pasta, so you'll be left with a spicy, mouth-numbing, fishy sauce that coats the noodles perfectly. If tilapia isn't your bag, sub with a different white, flaky fish like snapper, rainbow trout, or flounder.

HOT TIP ★ IN A PINCH, YOU CAN USE ANY KIND OF DRIED RED PEPPER FLAKES IN LIEU OF THE GOCHUGARU, BUT THE SICHUAN PEPPERCORNS ARE KINDA NONNEGOTIABLE.

1 pound tilapia fillets
2 tablespoons soy sauce
1 tablespoon finely grated fresh ginger
3 tablespoons Sichuan peppercorns
1 tablespoon gochugaru
Kosher salt
16 ounces spaghetti
⅓ cup extra-virgin olive oil
5 cloves garlic, roughly chopped
2 scallions, thinly sliced
2 tablespoons chopped fresh cilantro
Lemon wedges, for serving

1. Slice the tilapia against the grain into ¼-inch-thick slices. In a medium bowl, toss together the tilapia, soy sauce, and ginger. Marinate in the fridge for at least 30 minutes and up to 1 hour.

2. Using a high-powered blender, spice grinder, or mortar and pestle, smash the Sichuan peppercorns, gochugaru, and ½ teaspoon kosher salt together.

3. Bring a large pot of salted water to a boil over medium-high heat. Add the spaghetti and cook according to package directions.

4. Meanwhile, in a large skillet, heat the olive oil over low heat and add the peppercorn mixture. Cook for about 5 minutes, stirring occasionally, until fragrant. Increase the heat to medium-high, add the fish, and cook for 2 minutes. Add the garlic and cook until the fish is cooked through, 1 to 2 minutes longer. Transfer the fish and oil to a large bowl and season with salt.

5. Using tongs, transfer the cooked pasta to the fish mixture and stir vigorously to combine. Add up to ½ cup pasta water for a saucier pasta.

6. Top with scallions and cilantro and serve with lemon wedges.

SEVEN OF CUPS

FREEING DESIRE

Even when we feel we are open and in touch with our feelings, it can be difficult to pinpoint exactly what we desire. The clouds are parting to show you a clear picture of what truly lights you up inside. Appearances can be deceiving. A perceived longing for a big house may be a stand-in for the security you actually yearn for. Listen to your heart closely and be patient.

As you participate in this process of discovery, watch what you seem naturally attracted to and follow the thread to find its deeper meaning. For example, take your attraction to this crudo recipe—is it the fish or the magickal properties of the avocado and grapefruit you're after? Get into it and find out!

MAGICKAL INGREDIENTS: AVOCADO, GRAPEFRUIT, LEMON, CHIVES (SEE ALLIUMS)

CRUDO
WITH GRAPEFRUIT AND AVOCADO

SNACK —— SERVES 2

There are three things you need to know about this recipe. First, crudo is a simple Italian raw fish dish usually made with olive oil and some sort of citrus. Second, *don't make it unless* you can find premium fresh fish. Most reputable fishmongers will have some on hand, just call ahead and ask about the selection. Halibut, fluke, yellowtail, sea bream, or snapper would all work with the citrus notes here.

The third thing you need to know involves how you slice the fish. Don't be too precious about it. We aren't training to become the next Jiro (that would take decades!)—just do your best. You'll place the fish in the freezer for 15 minutes to firm up the meat before slicing. Then, you'll slice it thinly, on a diagonal, against the grain. We like the slices around ⅛ inch thick, but if you prefer a thicker cut, feel free to do so. Just don't slice it thicker than ¼ inch, or you'll run into some textural problems.

Oh, and if you can't find Meyer lemons, a regular lemon will totally work.

HOT TIP ★ TO SUPRÊME CITRUS, CUT THE ENDS OFF THE FRUIT, THEN USE A KNIFE TO SLICE THE PEEL OFF OF IT, REVEALING THE FRUIT WITHIN. MAKE SURE YOU GET ALL THE PITH AND MEMBRANE OFF. THEN SLICE ON EITHER SIDE OF THE FRUIT TO RELEASE IT FROM THE INNER MEMBRANES.

½ pound fresh fish of your choosing
1 grapefruit, supremed
Grated zest and juice of 1 Meyer lemon
1 avocado, halved and pitted
Flaky salt, such as Maldon
Extra-virgin olive oil, for drizzling
1 tablespoon thinly sliced fresh chives

1. Place the fish in the freezer for 15 minutes. Meanwhile, in a medium bowl, combine the grapefruit, lemon zest, and lemon juice. Use a spoon to scoop the avocado flesh in chunks into the bowl. Toss to coat.

2. Remove the fish from the freezer and slice it against the grain, on the diagonal, at an angle to the cutting board between ⅛ inch and ¼ inch thick.

3. Arrange the fish on a large plate and sprinkle with flaky salt. Drizzle with olive oil and spoon the avocado mixture over top. Top with the chives and more salt, if desired, and serve immediately.

EIGHT OF CUPS
EXPANDING EMPATHY

The lessons of the heart you've been gathering over the years are adding up to guide you in your quest to understand the motivations of others. Now it is time to turn that understanding inward. Extend the same kindness to yourself that you offer others. Give yourself the benefit of the doubt. Revisit past judgments with new empathy for yourself.

   You are collecting an upgraded box of emotional tools to carry with you into the next phase of your life. Make sure you are gathering those of the highest grade. Fit for a king even, just like these crab legs! And with the crab being the emblem for the most nurturing sign of the zodiac, this is truly a fitting symbolic feast.

MAGICKAL INGREDIENTS: GARLIC (SEE ALLIUMS), LEMON, TURMERIC

KING CRAB TEXAS TOAST ROLLS:
A LOVE STORY

MAIN —— SERVES 2 TO 3

Tackling king crab legs almost seems like an impossible feat, but they are super easy to cook—mostly because they've already been cooked by the time you get your hands on them! All you will need to do is heat them up. It's almost too easy . . . and *always* impressive.

   Another impressive thing about this recipe is the glory that is Texas toast. In its purest form, Texas toast is garlic bread made with thick white sandwich bread, but that can prove difficult to find when not in Texas, so any old white sandwich bread will do. Pile the crab on top of a slice, drizzle it with some garlic butter, aioli, and a spritz of lemon juice, fold the bread over on top of itself, and eat it like a crab roll. We fell in love with this recipe, and you will, too.

2 sticks (8 ounces) unsalted butter, melted

2 tablespoons minced garlic

4 teaspoons garlic powder

2½ teaspoons kosher salt

2 pounds steamed Alaskan King crab legs

8 slices thick-cut white bread

Aioli, store-bought or homemade turmeric aioli (page 48), for serving

Cocktail sauce, for serving

Lemon wedges, for serving

1. In a blender, combine the melted butter, garlic, garlic powder, and salt and blend on high for about 30 seconds.

2. Preheat the oven to 350°F. Pour ¼ inch of water into a large baking dish.

3. Add the crab legs to the baking dish and cover with foil. Bake for about 10 minutes to heat the crab legs through. Remove from the oven but leave the oven on and increase the temperature to 450°F.

4. Meanwhile, use a pastry brush to brush the garlic butter on one side of each slice of bread. Set aside the remaining garlic butter for serving. Arrange the bread on a baking sheet buttered-side up.

5. Transfer the bread to the oven and bake until toasted, about 4 minutes.

6. Use kitchen shears to snip right up the middle of the crab legs, revealing that sweet, sweet succulent meat. Throw the legs on a platter and serve with the leftover melted garlic butter, the aioli of your choice, cocktail sauce, lemon wedges, the Texas toast, and some frosty beers. Save yourself some work and tell everyone to assemble their own rolls.

NINE OF CUPS
RECEIVING SUPPORT

The emotional vulnerability you've practiced in one-on-one relationships is ready to expand. When you let it, you'll find that you have a multitude of sources of emotional support hiding right there in plain sight. Lean on them. That's what they're there for. If your companions become depleted, they'll take a break. Let them make that call for themselves.

Lime, which promotes attraction, can help you find the individuals and communities best suited to support you (and vice versa). Add chili powder for a boost of motivation and added passion for the project. You know what lime and chiles are good on? Oysters. We're going to have you shucking and grilling them like a pro. How's that for giving back to your supportive circle?

MAGICKAL INGREDIENTS: LIME, CHILE, GARLIC (SEE ALLIUMS)

GRILLED OYSTERS
WITH CHILI-LIME BUTTER

SNACK —— MAKES 1 DOZEN OYSTERS

Savoring a fresh, salty oyster is something everyone should experience at least once in their life. If you are averse to eating them raw, this recipe is a great step to get you there. The butter mellows the oyster's brininess and the chili-lime gives it the perfect pep.

If you are already a connoisseur, transform this simple recipe into a bona fide oyster extravaganza. Make a couple of different mignonettes and some cocktail sauce, along with the chili-lime butter recipe below (doubled or tripled, according to the size of your party). Then throw a bunch of oysters on ice next to some shucking knives and towels, pop open a few bottles of bubbles (preferably pét-nat) and let your guests shuck their own oysters and decide if they want to eat 'em raw or throw 'em on the grill.

HOT TIP ★ IF YOU DON'T HAVE A GRILL, OR JUST DON'T FEEL LIKE MESSING WITH IT, PLACE THE BUTTERED OYSTERS IN A SMALL RIMMED DISH (ON A BED OF ROCK SALT OR UNCOOKED RICE OR BEANS TO KEEP THEM FROM TIPPING OVER) AND PLACE THEM IN A 425°F OVEN UNTIL THE BUTTER MELTS AND THE JUICES START BUBBLING, ABOUT 8 MINUTES.

3 tablespoons unsalted butter, at room temperature

2 cloves garlic, minced

1 tablespoon fresh lime juice

2 teaspoons chili powder

1 dozen fresh oysters on the half shell

HOT TIP ★ THE TIME IT TAKES FOR THE OYSTERS TO COOK MAY VARY, DEPENDING ON THE HEAT OF YOUR GRILL. AN OYSTER IS DONE WHEN THE BUTTER HAS MELTED AND THE JUICES START TO BUBBLE UP. SOMETIMES THE OYSTER WILL EVEN JUMP UP OUT OF ITS SHELL AND DO A DANCE FOR YOU. (IT'S FROM ALL THEIR EXCITEMENT KNOWING HOW MUCH JOY THEY ARE ABOUT TO BRING TO THE PERSON WHO EATS THEM.)

1. Preheat the grill to high.

2. In a small bowl, thoroughly mix the butter, garlic, lime juice, and chili powder until completely incorporated.

3. Spoon 1 heaping teaspoon of the chili-lime butter mixture onto each oyster and place the oysters directly on the grill. Cook until the butter has melted and the juices begin to bubble, 7 to 10 minutes.

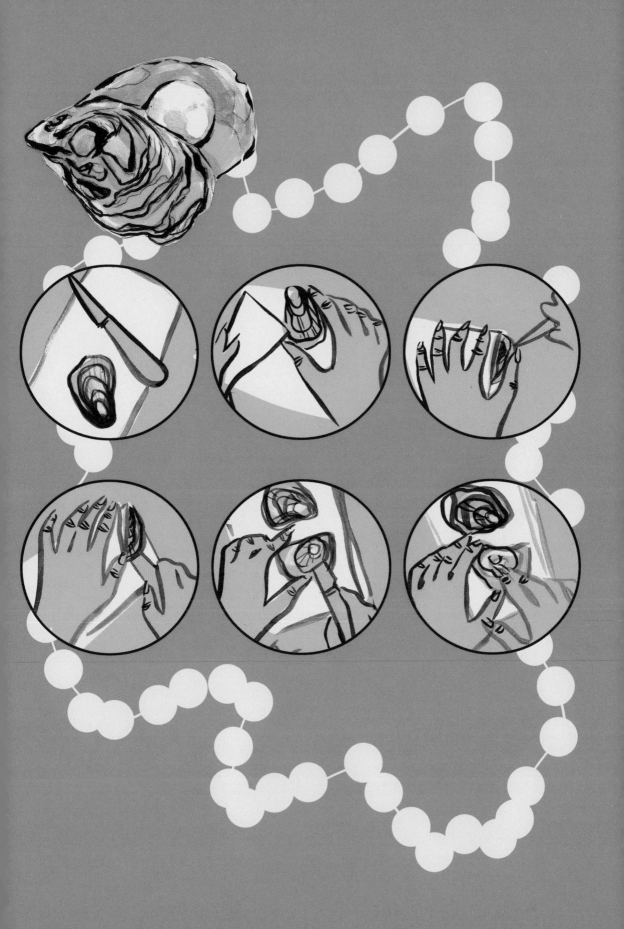

TEN OF CUPS
LOVING FREELY

It's the dawning of the age of Aquarius, baby! Ditch your restrictive civilian clothes and slip into something more comfortable—a caftan, maybe, or nothing at all. This level of love is freedom, pure and simple. To be accepted, supported, and celebrated by your community and to give all that goodness in return is golden.

Having this energy in your corner is so beautiful . . . almost as beautiful as this giant po'boy filled with blackened turbot. Okay, the pinnacle of collective love wins, but this giant sandwich is still pretty great. And it can feed your cohorts when they're tired out from all that naked dancing.

MAGICKAL INGREDIENTS: BLACK PEPPER, CAYENNE, GARLIC (SEE ALLIUMS), ONION (SEE ALLIUMS)

GIANT BLACKENED TURBOT PO'BOYS

MAIN —— SERVES 3 TO 4

The best bread for a po'boy is hard to find, because it pretty much only exists in Louisiana. So, what do we do? We PIVOT. Use a fluffy French loaf or a Vietnamese-style baguette—the same kind that's used for our Giant Banh Mis. Just don't use a traditional French baguette! The crust is too thick and chewy.

Serve these sandwiches up with some Zapp's potato chips and Sazerac cocktails and then, in classic Ten of Cups fashion, *laissez les bons temps rouler*.

HOT TIP ★ WHILE WE CALL FOR TURBOT, YOU CAN SWAP OUT FOR SNAPPER, SHRIMP, OR TILAPIA. THIS RECIPE MAKES TWO GIANT SANDWICHES, BUT IT CAN TOTALLY BE CUT IN HALF OR DOUBLED ACCORDING TO YOUR NEEDS.

2 French loaves (14 inches long)
1 tablespoon freshly ground black pepper
1 tablespoon freshly ground white pepper
1 tablespoon cayenne pepper
1 tablespoon garlic powder
1 tablespoon onion powder
1 tablespoon kosher salt
4 turbot fillets (8 ounces each)
3 tablespoons extra-virgin olive oil
1 cup mayonnaise
Louisiana-style hot sauce (optional), such as Crystal
1 small head iceberg lettuce, shredded
1 large tomato, thinly sliced
¾ cup dill pickle chips

1. Preheat the oven to 450°F.

2. Slice each loaf in half lengthwise and if the bread is very dense, scoop out some of the insides to make room for the filling. Put all 4 bread halves on a baking sheet and toast them in the oven until the edges start to crisp, 2 to 3 minutes. Remove the loaves from the oven and set aside.

3. In a small bowl, combine the black pepper, white pepper, cayenne, garlic powder, onion powder, and salt. Pat the turbot fillets dry and generously season them all over with the spice mixture.

4. Line a plate with paper towels and set down near the stove. In a large cast-iron or heavy-bottomed skillet, heat the oil over medium heat until it shimmers. Working in batches, add the turbot fillets and cook for about 4 minutes per side until blackened. Transfer the turbot to the paper towels as you work.

5. Slather both halves of each toasted loaf with the mayonnaise and add a few dashes of the hot sauce (if using). Add the fish, shredded lettuce, tomato, and pickles to the bottom halves of each loaf. Cover them with the top halves and press down slightly. Slice each sandwich in half or thirds and serve.

PAGE OF CUPS

EARTH OF WATER ★ RENEWING TRUST

Wash off the residue of heartaches past. A new day is dawning, opening you up to fresh emotional connections. If you sense yourself falling into old patterns or making assumptions based on past relationships, gently pull your attention to the here and now. Stay rooted in reality and your vulnerability will blossom.

Let the world see your needs; pay attention to who responds and how. Sometimes the simplest moves are the strongest. Like this stone fruit cobbler. Stone fruits are delicious—sweet, juicy, associated with love and sensuality. They get to shine in all their glory while getting cuddled by a perfect batter that supports who they are and never tries to make them into someone else. Perfect inspiration for your quest.

MAGICKAL INGREDIENT: STONE FRUIT

STONE FRUIT COBBLER

DESSERT —— SERVES 8 TO 10

This is a simple, delicious cobbler, plain as that. Hardly anything is done to the fruit—it's hand-crushed with a little bit of sugar and thickened with just a touch of flour. This makes for lots of small chunks of juicy fruit throughout, with a flavor that's clean and pristine. Almost like picking a ripe stone fruit from a tree and eating it in the shade . . . but with a deliciously delicate, cakey accessory.

We recommend using peaches, nectarines, plums, apricots, or mangos (or even persimmons if stone fruits are out of season). Just promise you won't make this with frozen fruit.

3½ pounds stone fruit

1 cup sugar

1 cup plus 3 tablespoons all-purpose flour

1 teaspoon baking powder

½ teaspoon kosher salt

1 stick (4 ounces) unsalted butter, melted and cooled to room temperature

½ cup whole milk

Buttermilk or vanilla ice cream (optional), store-bought or homemade (page 105)

1. Preheat the oven to 375°F. Grease a 9 × 13-inch baking pan.

2. Peel the fruit over a large bowl and reserve all the juices. Place the peeled fruit in a separate large bowl. Tear the fruit off of the pit, crushing it with your hands into 1-inch chunks, and add to the bowl of reserved juice. You should have about 6 cups of hand-crushed fruit. If you have significantly less or more of that, add or take away fruit as necessary. Add ¼ cup of the sugar and 3 tablespoons of the flour and toss to combine.

3. In a medium bowl, whisk together the remaining 1 cup flour, remaining ¾ cup sugar, the baking powder, and salt. Add the melted butter and milk and whisk to combine.

4. Pour half of the batter into the bottom of the baking pan. Top with the fruit mixture. Dollop the remaining batter on top of the fruit and use a knife to swirl the batter around (kind of like you are making cream cheese brownies).

5. Bake the cobbler until the batter is browned and crispy and the fruit starts to bubble, about 50 minutes. Let cool for 30 minutes before serving.

KNIGHT OF CUPS

FIRE OF WATER ★ OFFERING THE JEWEL

Your heart is reaching the boiling point, urging you to leave your comfort zone to find connection. Whether romantic, platonic, or familial, seeking out love—if we are to be successful—requires offering out our hearts. Yes, it means we risk being disappointed, but not taking the risk leaves us with that restless feeling forever, and doesn't that sound a lot worse?

Remember, you are leading with what you have to offer, not with what you desire from someone else. It can be difficult to tell the two apart. Vanilla, the magickal ingredient of The Lovers (see page 144), helps to attract the right people and lemon boosts the bonding factor. What a stroke of luck that both are featured in this citrus pudding cake!

MAGICKAL INGREDIENTS: VANILLA, LEMON

CITRUS PUDDING CAKE

DESSERT —— SERVES 6 TO 8

This cake is very much like a custard, yielding a super-moist, pudding consistency that is somehow also light and fluffy. It's magick! It comes together quickly and keeps well, making it the perfect dessert to throw together in the morning for a get-together later that night. Because of its custard-like qualities, you'll bake this cake in a water bath to keep the eggs from curdling.

Use any combination of citrus you like. Lemon is the classic move, but lime or grapefruit are also delicious. If you use a sweeter fruit, like orange or tangerine, be sure to cut it with a little bit of lemon or lime juice to balance the sweetness with some sour notes.

4 large eggs, separated

1½ cups whole milk

1 cup sugar

2 tablespoons unsalted butter, melted and cooled to room temperature

1 tablespoon grated citrus zest

6 tablespoons freshly squeezed citrus juice

1 teaspoon pure vanilla extract

½ teaspoon kosher salt

½ cup all-purpose flour

1. Preheat the oven to 350°F. Grease an 8-inch square or round baking dish.

2. Fill a large roasting pan less than halfway with water and place it in the oven. This is your water bath.

3. In a large bowl, whisk together the egg yolks, milk, sugar, butter, citrus zest, citrus juice, vanilla, and salt. Stir in the flour and whisk until there are no lumps.

4. In a stand mixer fitted with the whisk, whip the egg whites on high until soft peaks form. Spoon one-quarter of the egg whites into the batter and whisk until smooth. Using a spatula, fold the remaining egg whites into the batter and pour it all into the prepared baking dish.

5. Place the baking dish in the water bath in the oven and bake until a knife inserted into the center of the cake comes out clean, about 45 minutes.

HOT TIP ★ WHEN YOU PLACE THE BAKING DISH IN THE WATER BATH, MAKE SURE IT'S NOT FLOATING. IF IT FLOATS, YOU'LL NEED TO EMPTY SOME OF THE WATER OUT.

6. Remove the baking dish from the water bath, then carefully remove the water bath from the oven. Let the cake cool for about 10 minutes and serve warm or room temperature, scooping spoonfuls directly onto plates.

QUEEN OF CUPS

WATER OF WATER ★ SWIMMING IN FEELINGS

If you're a naturally emotional person, this energy is heaven. If you are not, get ready for a wild ride! Once you sink in, let go and give in to the movement. Old feelings revisit with no explanation, new ones inhabit your body to give you a taste of the future. You are being cleansed and saturated in the language of your heart. Get fluent.

We're so serious about getting you into the aqueous spirit that we couldn't make this recipe solid. Its liquid form is part of the spell. Sarsaparilla and sassafras team up to keep you protected, while clove, cinnamon, and ginger conspire to make you the most confident, mood-lifting magician the world has ever known. Use liberally and irresponsibly.

MAGICKAL INGREDIENTS: SARSAPARILLA, SASSAFRAS,
CLOVE, GINGER, CINNAMON, ORANGE

ROOT BEER ELIXIR FLOAT

DESSERT —— SERVES 8

In typical fashion, the syrup used for this root beer float gets its flavor from sassafras and sarsaparilla, but it's the addition of ginger and a few other secret ingredients that takes it above and beyond any root beer you've ever tasted. In addition to making it into a float, as here, you can just add sparkling water to make a soda. You could also use it to flavor up a fancy cocktail in place of simple syrup or drizzle it all over the Croissant Bread Pudding (page 55).

Zest strips from 1 orange
2-inch piece fresh ginger, sliced
2 tablespoons sassafras bark
1 tablespoon sarsaparilla root
5 whole cloves
1 whole star anise
1 cinnamon stick
2 cups granulated sugar
½ teaspoon pure vanilla extract
¼ teaspoon kosher salt
1 liter sparkling water or club soda
Buttermilk or vanilla ice cream, store-bought or homemade (optional; page 105)

1. In a medium pot, combine 2 cups water, the orange peel, ginger, sassafras, sarsaparilla, cloves, star anise, and cinnamon and bring to a boil over medium-high heat. Once boiling, remove from the heat, cover, and let steep at room temperature for 1 hour or up to overnight.

2. Strain the liquid through a fine-mesh sieve (discard the solids). Return the liquid to the pot and bring to a boil over medium-high heat. Add the sugar, vanilla, and salt and stir until the sugar has dissolved completely, about 1 minute. Store in an airtight container in the fridge for up to 1 month.

3. For each float, add ¼ cup of the syrup and ½ cup of sparkling water to a frosted glass. Stir to combine and add 1 or 2 scoops of ice cream.

KING OF CUPS

The art of feeling emotions fully without getting overwhelmed is being revealed to you now. Often clouded in mystery, this elusive practice takes, well, practice. A vessel sailing on the sea may float on the water, but it still feels the waves. We often try to be airplanes instead, flying above, unaffected. This robs us of compassion. Keep communication with your heart open and your gaze fixed on the horizon.

As you hone your skill, your vessel may take on some water now and then. Don't panic. Simply pour those feelings back into the ocean and continue. The methodical churning of the waves is the perfect soundtrack to making this buttermilk ice cream. Embrace the decadence. You've earned it after all that heart work.

MAGICKAL INGREDIENT: VANILLA

BUTTERMILK ICE CREAM

DESSERT —— MAKES 2 PINTS

It may seem strange—adding buttermilk to ice cream—but it adds an incredibly tasty tang that takes plain old vanilla up a notch.

The trick here is not to bring the mixture all the way to a boil, because the eggs will curdle, rendering your classic crème anglaise base useless. Since you'll be freezing this into ice cream, err on the side of caution and remove it from the heat sooner rather than later. You'll add the cold buttermilk at the very end to keep the mixture from overheating, then chill it for a few hours before spinning it into ice cream.

HOT TIP ★ IF YOU DO ACCIDENTALLY BOIL THE CREAM AND CURDLE THE EGGS, THERE IS NO COMING BACK. YOU'LL HAVE TO START OVER WITH A NEW BATCH.

2 cups heavy cream

1 vanilla bean, split lengthwise, or 2 teaspoons vanilla extract

¾ cup sugar

6 large egg yolks

½ teaspoon kosher salt

1 cup whole buttermilk

1. Place the cream in a medium saucepan. If using a vanilla bean, scrape the seeds out of the pod with the back of the knife into the cream and add the pod, too. If using extract, simply add to the cream. Bring to a boil over medium-high heat, then remove the pot from the heat.

2. In a large bowl, whisk together the sugar, egg yolks, and salt until the mixture is thick and pale yellow. Whisk in the hot cream mixture until fully combined, then return the mixture to the saucepan. Heat over low heat until it thickens and coats the back of a spoon, about 3 minutes, being careful not to bring to a boil. Remove from the heat and immediately whisk in the buttermilk until fully combined.

3. Strain the mixture through a fine-mesh sieve into a large pitcher. Cover it with plastic wrap and refrigerate for at least 3 hours and up to overnight to chill.

4. Pour the chilled mixture into an ice cream maker and churn according to the manufacturer's instructions. Remove the ice cream using a spatula and transfer to an airtight container to freeze completely, 2 to 3 hours.

IF YOU DON'T OWN AN ICE CREAM MAKER AND HAVE NO INTEREST IN BUYING ONE, NEVER FEAR! YOU CAN STILL MAKE THIS ICE CREAM. BE WARNED, THE TEXTURE WON'T BE AS CREAMY, BUT IT WILL STILL TASTE DELICIOUS.

ALL YOU HAVE TO DO IS POUR THE CHILLED CREAM MIXTURE INTO A 1-GALLON ZIP-TOP FREEZER BAG. (DOUBLE-LINE IT AS INSURANCE AGAINST SPILLAGE.) PUT THE BAG IN THE FREEZER AND CLEAR YOUR SCHEDULE BECAUSE YOU AREN'T GOING ANYWHERE FOR A WHILE. EVERY HOUR AND A HALF, REMOVE THE BAG FROM THE FREEZER AND SQUISH THE CREAM AROUND. THIS INCORPORATES AIR AND DISCOURAGES LARGE ICE CRYSTALS FROM FORMING. IT'S ABOUT AS CLOSE TO CHURNED AS YOU ARE GONNA GET WITHOUT AN ACTUAL ICE CREAM MACHINE. KEEP DOING THIS FOR AT LEAST 6 HOURS, OR UNTIL THE ICE CREAM FREEZES FULLY.

COINS

EARTH ★ VEGGIES + GRAINS

HOME, FINANCE, PHYSICALITY

Coins carry the power of Elemental Earth. While the name "Coins" leads some to think that this suit is all about money and career, it's about so much more. If you can touch it, smell it, mold it with your hands, or lay your head down on it to sleep at night, it comes from Earth energy. Earth can sometimes be the most difficult element to describe because it's so much a part of us. It's like trying to explain water to a fish. Even our bodies are a manifestation of this energy, being the physical home of our spiritual selves.

　　We can alter our experience of being in our bodies with what we put into them and how we use them. We've got some inspiration to get you started. Dig your hands into these ten vegetablecentric recipes, then taste the sweet rewards of the nobles of Earth. Kick off your shoes, put a flower behind your ear and a garnet in your overalls, and let's get to work.

ACE OF COINS
ACCEPTING THE GIFT OF EARTH

You are a child of Earth. You and everyone you know has evolved to exist in exactly this environment, to live in harmony with the world around you. Get into it. Your body was made to survive in these precise conditions, now it's time to get the rest of you attuned to the frequency of Earth. Open yourself to the knowledge that you can form your own world like clay in your hands.

It takes practice to move mountains, but you're up for it. Making use of every last bit of bounty the Earth provides is a surefire way to let the Universe know you fully honor all that she offers. So, stop throwing away your vegetable scraps and make this broth out of them instead!

MAGICKAL INGREDIENT: ONIONS (SEE ALLIUMS), CELERY

VEGETABLE STOCK

BACK POCKET BASIC —— MAKES ABOUT 4 CUPS

Use this recipe exactly as written, or as inspiration for a stock of your very own. The move is to keep a large zip-top bag in the freezer and every time you cook something, add all the vegetable scraps to it. Once you have enough scraps saved up, throw them in a pot, cover them with water, and make the broth.

Onion, carrot, and celery are the most commonly used vegetables in broths of this nature, but you can add any vegetable you like: bell pepper, garlic, tomato, leek, mushroom, parsnip, ginger, and herbs. Even Parmigiano cheese rinds!

HOT TIPS:

★ THE VEGETABLES YOU USE WILL MOST CERTAINLY IMPART FLAVOR TO THE BROTH. SO, IF YOU DON'T LIKE THE TASTE OF FENNEL, DON'T PUT ANY IN YOUR VEGETABLE STOCK.

★ POTATOES AND THEIR PEELS WILL ACT AS A THICKENER, SO DON'T GO OVERBOARD WITH THEM.

★ IT'S TOTALLY COOL TO LEAVE THE SKINS ON THE ONIONS AND GARLIC, IT ADDS EVEN MORE FLAVOR.

★ IF YOU REALLY WANT TO MAKE A SHOW OF IT, ROAST YOUR SCRAPS FIRST OR SAUTÉ THEM IN THE POT BEFORE ADDING WATER.

★ WAIT TO SEASON THE STOCK UNTIL YOU KNOW WHAT YOU ARE GOING TO BE USING IT IN, THEN SEASON TO TASTE.

The main thing you should understand is to do what feels right. Use the vegetables you love, in amounts that make sense to you, keeping in mind that if you use all of one vegetable, like an onion, you'll be making onion stock, not vegetable stock, so be balanced in your selection.

1 large yellow onion, unpeeled, roughly chopped

2 large carrots, roughly chopped

2 celery ribs, roughly chopped

1. In a large stockpot, combine the onion, carrots, and celery (or whatever else you've stocked up on) and add water to cover by 2 inches. Bring to a simmer over medium-high heat, cover, reduce the heat to low, and cook until the water is deeply infused, about 1 hour.

2. Strain the stock through a fine-mesh sieve (discard the solids). Store in an airtight container in the fridge for up to 1 week or in the freezer for 3 months.

TWO OF COINS
PLANTING SEEDS

You may not be able to see it yet, but you are standing on a future empire. The resources you have now are exactly what you need to build your grand vision. If the final details are hazy, that's okay. Keep tabs on the direction you're headed and adjust as needed. An oak sapling has no idea how many branches it will grow, but it does know it has to go up.

All root vegetables are excellent for grounding, but the potato is the ruler of them all. Endlessly malleable, it's the exact sort of ally you want by your side at the start of a new project. Get cozy with your taters by adding tots to this hotdish. Congrats! You're officially Minnesotan.

MAGICKAL INGREDIENTS: POTATOES, ONION (SEE ALLIUMS), BLACK PEPPER

BROCCOLI AND CHEESE TATER CASSEROLE
WITH CAULIFLOWER RICE

SIDE —— SERVES 4 TO 6

Casseroles have a bad rep in the professional food world. Let's face it: The vegetables are often overcooked, there is never a perfect sear on any meat involved, and the only thing melting in your mouth is the gooey processed cheese. AND WE ARE HERE FOR ALL OF IT.

A typical cafeteria-style broccoli and cheese casserole consists of canned soups, tons of cheese, frozen broccoli, and white rice all stuffed into a baking dish and baked to golden-brown perfection. For this recipe, you'll make a roux-based cheese sauce from scratch, and you'll use cauliflower rice in lieu of plain white rice. In many ways, this casserole is actually healthy!

There is a surprise ingredient at the end, too: TATER TOTS. This addition (Melinda's idea) is based on a casserole from Minnesota (Melinda's homeland) called Tater-Tot Hotdish. (As if we needed *another* reason to love the great state of Minnesota!)

1 large head cauliflower (about 2 pounds), broken into florets
2 tablespoons unsalted butter
2 tablespoons extra-virgin olive oil
1 cup diced white or yellow onion
Kosher salt and freshly ground black pepper
2 tablespoons all-purpose flour
1 cup whole milk
2 slices American cheese

2 cups shredded cheddar cheese
1 head broccoli (about 1 pound), broken into small florets
1 (16-ounce) bag frozen tater puffs

1. Preheat the oven to 350°F.

2. Working in batches, add the cauliflower to a food processor and pulse until a rice-like consistency forms.

HOT TIP ★ IF YOU DON'T HAVE A FOOD PROCESSOR, RICE THE WHOLE HEAD OF CAULIFLOWER ON THE LARGE HOLES OF A BOX GRATER.

3. In a 10-inch ovenproof skillet, heat the butter and oil over medium-high heat. When the butter has melted, increase the heat to high and add the onion and cauliflower rice and cook, stirring occasionally, until a crust starts to form on the bottom of the pan, about 10 minutes.

4. Season with salt and pepper to taste. Add the flour to the skillet and stir to combine and cook, stirring constantly, for 1 minute more. Reduce the heat to low and pour in the milk, stirring vigorously. Increase the heat to medium and bring the mixture to a boil. Add the American cheese and 1½ cups of the cheddar and stir until the cheese is melted and fully combined. Stir in the broccoli and remove from heat. Taste and season with salt and pepper as needed.

5. Flatten the mixture so it is evenly spread throughout the skillet and add the Tater Tots in a single layer on top. Sprinkle the remaining cheddar on top and bake until the cheese bubbles around the edges and the tots are browned, about 30 minutes. Let cool for 10 minutes before serving.

THREE OF COINS

FORMING ALLIANCES

You're ready to invite some fresh energy into your life. Though you don't have the skills to do everything required to reach your goals, you can find others who can help. Be on the lookout for people who are adept at things you have less experience with. Bring them into your circle. Even if they're not the best fit for what you've got going on now, they could prove to be an essential resource later on.

    Working with others is not always easy, but when it clicks, there's nothing better. Take these pot stickers: They bring baked potatoes, all the fixin's, and pot stickers together into one beautiful form. They're the perfect vehicle for showing off what great versatility you bring to the table.

MAGICKAL INGREDIENTS: POTATO, SCALLION (SEE ALLIUMS), GARLIC (SEE ALLIUMS), BLACK PEPPER

LOADED BAKED POTATO POT STICKERS

SIDE —— MAKES 18 POT STICKERS

That's right, we took the best things about a loaded baked potato (i.e., everything) and stuffed them inside gyoza wrappers. As noted, this recipe makes 18 pot stickers, which will serve 2 as a main, 4 as a side, or 1 if you are Courtney.

    The dipping sauce is a play on the black vinegar sauce you typically eat with dumplings, except with apple cider vinegar and a dollop of sour cream, because what's a loaded baked potato without a dollop of the good stuff?

HOT TIP ★ IF YOU CAN'T FIND GYOZA OR DUMPLING WRAPPERS, WONTON WRAPPERS WORK. INSTEAD OF FOLDING THEM INTO HALF-MOONS, YOU'LL FOLD THEM INTO TRIANGLES.

DIPPING SAUCE

2 tablespoons sour cream

2 tablespoons soy sauce

2 teaspoons apple cider vinegar

2 tablespoons finely chopped scallion greens

POT STICKERS

1 (12- to 14-ounce) russet (baking) potato, peeled and quartered

2 slices bacon, cooked and finely chopped

⅓ cup shredded cheddar cheese

1 tablespoon finely chopped scallion whites

½ teaspoon minced garlic

½ teaspoon kosher salt

¼ teaspoon freshly ground black pepper

1 (10-ounce) package gyoza or dumpling wrappers

1 tablespoon canola or vegetable oil

1. **MAKE THE DIPPING SAUCE:** In a small bowl, combine the sour cream, soy sauce, vinegar, and scallion greens. Refrigerate to chill.

2. **MAKE THE POT STICKERS:** Boil the potato until fork-tender, about 15 minutes. Drain and return to the pot. Reduce the heat to medium-low for about 1 minute to cook off excess water. Remove from the heat and smash with a potato masher or a fork until smooth. Let cool for 15 minutes.

3. In a medium bowl, combine the bacon, cheddar, scallion whites, garlic, salt, and black pepper. Add the potatoes and mix until fully combined. Add salt and pepper to taste.

4. To assemble the pot stickers, lay the wrappers out on a clean work surface. Working with one wrapper a time, spoon a rounded teaspoon of filling onto the center. Using a pastry brush or your fingers, brush water around the edges, then fold the wrapper over the filling to create a half-moon, pinching the edges together to seal and crimp. Repeat with the remaining filling and wrappers.

5. In a medium nonstick skillet, heat the oil over medium heat. When the oil shimmers, add all of the pot stickers in an even layer and cook, without turning, until the bottoms are golden brown, 2 to 3 minutes. Carefully pour in ½ cup water and immediately cover with a tight-fitting lid. Reduce the heat to medium-low and steam the pot stickers until the wrappers have softened, 3 to 4 minutes. Uncover the pan, and cook until most of the water has evaporated, 3 to 4 minutes.

6. Serve immediately with the dipping sauce.

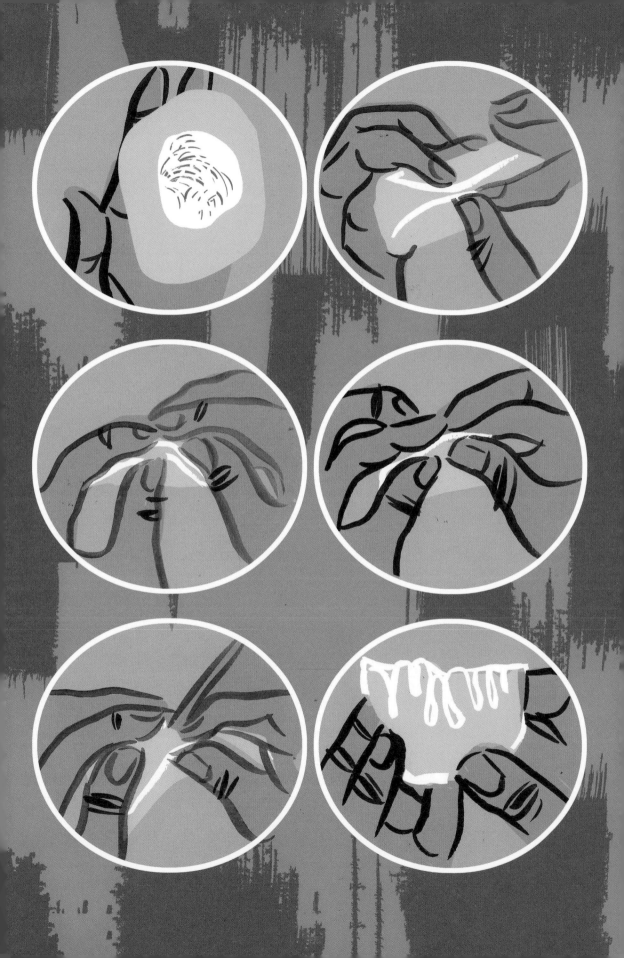

FOUR OF COINS
STANDING FIRM

You're planted on solid ground at last. Take a moment to feel the effects of the work you've done to create a life that supports your needs. Remember this sensation. This is the minimum level of stability you'll want to have long-term. Log it, but don't become consumed by it.

Security is wonderful to have at your center, but you can't remain wrapped in it or you'll never grow. Get ready to kick yourself out of the nest, but not before you're fully recharged. Get the ball rolling with these pickles. Dill and mustard seed fortify the mind, so you won't get lured off track, and that old workhorse garlic gets needed spiritual cleansing done.

MAGICKAL INGREDIENTS: DILL, MUSTARD SEED, GARLIC (SEE ALLIUMS)

PICKLED VEGGIES

BACK POCKET BASIC —— MAKES 1 PINT

You are looking at a recipe for a basic brine that will pickle any vegetable. Our go-to combination of vinegar is ⅓ cup each of apple cider vinegar, sherry vinegar, and distilled vinegar.

That said, play around with different vinegars and flavorings to add to the jar. If you are pickling turnips, beets, or fennel, maybe use champagne vinegar and add a cinnamon stick or a few cloves. If you like spice, add some chiles. If you don't like garlic or dill, don't add it. The point is, you have options and there is no wrong answer.

You'll need enough chopped vegetables to tightly fill a 16-ounce container and you can pickle pretty much any kind you want. Cucumbers get the most press, of course, but try carrots, peppers, green beans, onions, okra, or sugar snap peas, too. Once you've picked your pickle, follow the instructions below and you'll be made in the shade.

Put these on the table to make any meal complete.

2 cups vegetable of your choosing (cut into ¼- to ½-inch-thick pieces)

3 sprigs dill

1 garlic clove, smashed and peeled

¼ teaspoon mustard seeds

⅓ cup sherry vinegar

⅓ cup apple cider vinegar

⅓ cup distilled white vinegar

1 tablespoon sugar

2¼ teaspoons kosher salt

1. Pack the vegetable, dill, garlic, and mustard seeds into a 16-ounce jar or airtight container.

2. In a small pot, combine the vinegars, sugar, salt, and ¾ cup water and bring to a boil over medium-high heat. Carefully pour the liquid over the vegetables until completely covered. Discard any extra liquid.

3. Seal the container and refrigerate for 3 days to pickle. Once pickled, the vegetables only get better with every day that passes. Store in the fridge for up to 1 month.

FIVE OF COINS
OVERCOMING SCARCITY

Resource management is tough work, so why do we make it harder for ourselves? Obsessing about what we don't have is the real great American pastime (sorry, baseball!). The problem, besides how terrible it feels, is that it takes up a *lot* of energy that could be spent focused on building with what we have and identifying our true needs. Slay the scarcity-mentality vampire with—what else? Garlic.

Garlic gets a lotta play, but this is truly its time to shine. In addition to repelling vampires, it is used in protection, driving away evil, and energy clearing spells in many folk medicine and magickal traditions. There is a TON of it in this recipe. Be gone, energy suckers!

MAGICKAL INGREDIENTS: GARLIC (SEE ALLIUMS), LEMON, MUSHROOMS, RADISH, ENDIVE (SEE CHICORIES), RADICCHIO (SEE CHICORIES), CELERY, FENNEL, POTATOES

BAGNA CAUDA "CRUDITÉS" FONDUE

SNACK —— SERVES 8 TO 10

Bagna cauda is a traditional dish from Piedmont, Italy, and if you've never tried it, now is your chance. Technically a dip, it's really more like an oil fondue. You'll also add some preserved lemons, which are for sure *not* a traditional Piedmontese ingredient (they are typically found in North African cuisine), but they add wonderful sour notes to amplify the flavors of the garlic oil and anchovy.

Serve the bagna cauda with some crusty bread and an assortment of fresh and cooked vegetables (we call them "crudités" for ease), and everyone can either use their hands or a skewer to dip the veggies into the oil. If you have a fondue pot, now would be a fabulous time to bust it out.

BAGNA CAUDA

1 cup extra-virgin olive oil

2 whole heads garlic, roughly chopped

1 (3.17-ounce) jar anchovies in oil

½ preserved lemon, roughly chopped

ACCOMPANIMENTS

3 pounds assorted crudités of your choosing (see page 116 for suggestions)

1 large loaf crusty bread, cut into ¼-inch slices, for serving

1. **MAKE THE BAGNA CAUDA:** In a large saucepan, combine the olive oil, garlic, anchovies, and lemon and heat over low heat for 30 minutes, until fragrant. Using a spoon or potato masher, mash the mixture into a paste. Cook, mashing occasionally, until the anchovies and garlic have basically melted into the oil and it is deeply fragrant, 2 to 3 hours longer.

HOT TIP ★ IF THE OIL IS TOO HOT, IT WILL COOK EVERYTHING TOO FAST AND THE RESULT WON'T BE AS TASTY. THE OIL SHOULD JUST BARELY BUBBLE AS YOU SLOWLY DISSOLVE EVERYTHING INTO IT.

2. Meanwhile, prepare the crudités. Choose one to two each of raw, broiled, and boiled veggies. Our go-tos are raw endive and radishes, broiled trumpet mushrooms and shishito peppers, boiled potatoes, and blanched broccolini.

3. Arrange the crudités on a large platter with the warm bagna cauda in the center and serve with bread.

4. **FOR THE RAW VEGETABLES:** Wash them well, remove the stems, and separate any leaves. Submerge in ice water for a few minutes to make them extra crisp.

5. **FOR THE BROILED VEGETABLES:** Set the broiler to high. Working with one vegetable at a time toss each with olive oil and kosher salt and arrange on a sheet pan, being sure not to overcrowd the pan. Broil until charred, about 5 minutes.

6. **FOR THE BOILED POTATOES:** Add the potatoes to a pot of water and bring to a boil over medium-high heat. Boil until tender, about 25 minutes.

7. To blanch asparagus, Romanesco, broccolini, and cauliflower, bring a pot of water to a boil over medium-high heat. Once boiling, add each vegetable separately and cook until just softened, about 3 minutes. Remove them from the pot using tongs, add to a large bowl, and immediately run under cold water.

SUGGESTED "CRUDITÉS"

RAW

★ greens (like kale, chard, mustard, radicchio, endive, or Little Gem lettuce)

★ 1 small bunch radishes, whole or halved

★ celery ribs, cut into bite-size pieces

BROILED

★ carrots, cut into bite-size pieces

★ turnips, cut into bite-size pieces

★ fennel bulb, cut into bite-size pieces

★ large mushrooms, whole or halved

★ zucchini, cut into bite-size pieces

★ whole shishito peppers

BOILED OR BLANCHED

★ fingerling potatoes, halved

★ whole, trimmed asparagus

★ Romanesco, broken into florets

★ whole, trimmed broccolini

★ cauliflower, broken into florets

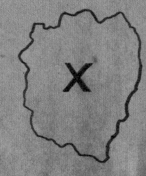

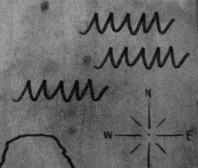

SIX OF COINS
RECOGNIZING ACCOMPLISHMENT

Look at all you've built with those capable hands! Put down your tools, step back, and take it all in. A necessary part of any project is reflecting on what went well, what didn't, and how you recovered when it didn't. Little moves made in the moment show themselves as genius improvisations when seen from a distance.

When things come easy to us, we might not recognize the value of our own skill. Make sure you're seeing yourself clearly, and your work for what it is. You're gonna need some discernment—the lemon will help with that. Then, once your magickal and creative abilities are lit up by the cinnamon and fennel in these sweet potatoes, it will all seem both valuable and easy.

MAGICKAL INGREDIENTS: CINNAMON, FENNEL, LEMON, PECANS

SMASHED SWEET POTATOES
WITH PECAN DUKKAH

SIDE —— SERVES 2 TO 4

This is not—in any way—an authentic dukkah recipe, but regardless of its lack of authenticity, it's still important to thank the people of the culture that invented this nutty spice blend that goes great on pretty much everything: the Egyptians!

This "dukkah" has a Southern American twist, with pecans instead of the usual hazelnuts or pistachios. And don't be fooled by the addition of cinnamon and allspice, spices that are commonly found in sweeter dishes—the only sugary sweetness here is what occurs naturally in the potatoes.

Speaking of naturally occurring sugars, the most important part of this recipe is the slow, low cooking time. It allows all those natural sugars to caramelize. And with the addition of lemon juice at the end to counteract the sweet notes, well, we'd like to think it would make the Egyptians proud.

4 sweet potatoes (5 to 6 ounces each)
⅓ cup halved pecans
1 teaspoon fennel seeds
¼ teaspoon ground cinnamon
¼ teaspoon ground allspice
½ teaspoon kosher salt
4 tablespoons (2 ounces) unsalted butter
1 lemon, cut into wedges
Flaky salt, such as Maldon, for serving

1. Preheat the oven to 350°F.

2. Wrap each potato in foil and place directly on the oven rack. Bake until soft, 45 minutes to 1 hour. Halve the potatoes lengthwise. Don't slice them all the way through, keep the halves connected.

3. Meanwhile, in a food processor or high-powered blender, combine the pecans, fennel seeds, cinnamon, allspice, and salt and pulse until coarsely chopped.

4. In a large nonstick or cast-iron skillet, melt the butter over low heat. Sprinkle the nut mixture evenly over the melted butter, then place each sweet potato in the skillet, cut-side down. Using a large spoon or metal spatula, press down on the sweet potatoes to flatten them so they cover the surface area of the entire skillet. Increase the heat to medium-low and cook, spooning the butter over the potatoes, until the bottoms are browned and caramelized, about 10 minutes.

5. Remove the pan from the heat and carefully invert the potatoes onto a platter, browned-side up. You can do this in one fell swoop or take them out one at a time and place them on the platter. Squeeze some lemon and a sprinkle of big, flaky salt on top and serve with the remaining lemon wedges.

SEVEN OF COINS
TRUSTING THE WORK

So. You've been passed over for promotion. Again. Or your book hasn't gotten picked up, your tour got canceled, they skipped your song at karaoke. Whatever is making you doubt yourself is not a real indication of the quality of your work or how hard you've labored. So, where does that leave you? What do you do?

Trust the work. That's it. That's the magick. Give it the benefit of the doubt. It's working even if you can't see the results just yet. And if you still have doubts, we've got a little more help for you starting with the oregano in these ranch-style *magick* beans to pry open your defeated heart.

MAGICKAL INGREDIENTS: OREGANO, BEANS, CUMIN, CAYENNE, CHILE, ONION (SEE ALLIUMS), BLACK PEPPER, LIME, GARLIC (SEE ALLIUMS)

A BIG OL' CAULDRON OF RANCH-STYLE BEANS

SIDE —— MAKES 8 CUPS

What makes these beans ranch-style? Well, it's mostly the zesty spices but also the hardworking attitude you have when you make them. Just like any rancher will tell you, it's not about the destination, it's about the long road to get there. And for this journey, that means you don't get to use canned beans, you have to start with dried. The good news is it's not really that much extra work. You just need to know you are making them at least a day in advance so you can soak them overnight.

Beef broth is used for the classic version of ranch-style beans, but Vegetable Stock (see page 108) works great if you'd prefer to keep it vegetarian. Alternatively, if you want it extra meaty, throw some bacon or a ham hock in the pot while the beans are boiling. For a full meal, serve the beans over some rice with a dollop of sour cream.

HOT TIP ★ THE CAYENNE GIVES THIS DISH QUITE A KICK, SO IF YOU DON'T WANT SPICY BEANS, OMIT IT OR CUT IT IN HALF.

3 tablespoons extra-virgin olive oil

1 large white or yellow onion, diced

3 tablespoons chili powder

1 teaspoon ground cumin

1 teaspoon cayenne pepper (optional)

7 garlic cloves, roughly chopped

6 cups Bone Broth (page 58) or store-bought beef broth

1 pound dried pinto beans, soaked overnight and drained

1 cup canned tomato puree

½ teaspoon dried oregano

1 teaspoon seasoned salt, such as Lawry's

1 tablespoon light brown sugar

1 lime, halved

Kosher salt and freshly ground black pepper

1. In a large pot, heat the olive oil over medium heat. When the oil shimmers, add the onion, chili powder, cumin, and cayenne (if using) and sauté until the onion is soft and fragrant, about 5 minutes. Add the garlic and sauté for 2 minutes more.

2. Add the broth and scrape any browned bits off the bottom of the pot. Add the beans and bring to a boil over high heat. Once boiling, reduce the heat to low, cover, and simmer for 1 hour, stirring occasionally, to give the beans a head start on cooking.

3. Add the tomato puree, oregano, seasoned salt, brown sugar, and lime halves to the pot and simmer, uncovered, until the beans are soft and the sauce has thickened, about 1 hour longer. Remove the pot from the heat. Pull out the lime halves and squeeze the juice into the pot. Season with salt and pepper to taste. Cool 10 minutes before serving.

EIGHT OF COINS
BUILDING A LEGACY

You know how people talk about buying a house they can grow into? Something that is great now but also allows for growth in the future? Look at the structure of your life and whether it will suit you five or ten years from now. Does your environment accommodate your ideal life? Can the city you live in support your career goals? Does your money management need a tune-up? Take care of it.

Lemon and cumin team up to give you clarity into what you can happily and realistically commit to. Dill brings that plan into sharper focus. You see why we made something you could reasonably eat for breakfast? Get a jump on your day and the rest of your life just by eating green eggs.

MAGICKAL INGREDIENTS: LEMON, CUMIN, DILL, PARSLEY, CILANTRO, CHIVES (SEE ALLIUMS), LEEKS (SEE ALLIUMS)

GREEN EGGS, NO HAM

SIDE —— SERVES 6

Green Eggs, No Ham gets its signature color from all the collards and herbs that are jam-packed into it. The trick to getting it right is in the eggs, which you'll cook like you are making a frittata or a *kuku sabzi*—a delicious, herbed-up Persian egg dish. The goal is to cook the eggs just enough to set, yet still remain soft and delicate.

Once they're done, you will love to eat them in the rain, on a train, near Nantucket, in a bucket, with Stevie Nicks, in brand-new kicks, on a branch, at the ranch, or pretty much anywhere, really.

CUMIN YOGURT

½ cup whole-milk plain Greek yogurt
1 tablespoon fresh lemon juice
¼ teaspoon ground cumin
¼ teaspoon kosher salt

FRITTATA

5 tablespoons extra-virgin olive oil
2 small leeks, finely chopped
Kosher salt
2 large bunches collard greens, stems and midribs removed, leaves roughly chopped
¼ cup finely chopped fresh dill
¼ cup finely chopped fresh Italian parsley
¼ cup finely chopped fresh cilantro
8 large eggs, beaten
Freshly ground black pepper
Thinly sliced chives, for serving

1. **MAKE THE CUMIN YOGURT:** In a small bowl, combine the yogurt, lemon juice, cumin, and salt.

2. **MAKE THE FRITTATA:** Heat a 10-inch ovenproof skillet over medium-low heat. Add 3 tablespoons of the oil and the leeks. Cook, stirring occasionally, until the leeks are soft and translucent, about 15 minutes. Season them with salt to taste.

3. Increase the heat to medium and add the collards in two batches, letting the first batch cook down for about 5 minutes. Add the second batch to the first and sauté, stirring often, until wilted, about 5 minutes more. Add the dill, parsley, cilantro, and 2 cups water and cook until most of the water has evaporated, about 30 minutes.

4. When cool enough to handle, transfer the mixture to a cutting board or food processor and chop to small pieces. Taste and season with salt as needed.

5. Preheat the oven to 400°F.

6. Return the greens to the skillet, add the remaining 2 tablespoons oil, and heat over medium heat. Add the eggs to the skillet and season with salt and pepper. Stir until the eggs start to thicken and set, about 4 minutes. Reduce the heat to medium-low and cook without stirring to form a crust on the bottom, about 3 minutes.

7. Transfer the skillet to the oven and bake until the eggs have set, about 5 more minutes. Invert the frittata onto a platter immediately or serve it straight from the pan. Let cool before serving, then spread the cumin yogurt in a thin layer over the top and garnish with chives.

NINE OF COINS
DEVELOPING SKILLS

Take out a notebook and pencil. School is in session. What you study is up to you. Online courses, grad school, certifications, finally reading that book on cultivating fruit trees for beginners that's been staring at you for months, whatever. What really matters is that you choose something that is valuable for the future you want to build and reasonable for you to take on right now.

If you still don't have any ideas, we can help you get there. Eggplant attracts abundance and success; it teams up with oregano to make sure your efforts align with your heart. Plus, everything gets layered up—just like the knowledge and skills you're going to be showing off in no time.

MAGICKAL INGREDIENTS: EGGPLANT, OREGANO, ONION (SEE ALLIUMS), CHILE, PARSLEY, RED PEPPER FLAKES (SEE CHILES), GARLIC (SEE ALLIUMS)

SMOKY EGGPLANT AND QUINOA

SIDE —— SERVES 4

As the quinoa in this dish bakes, it will soak up the spicy, savory eggplant sauce and puff up while a top layer of cheese gets golden brown, resulting in something like a cross between an eggplant quinoa bowl and baked pasta alla Norma. Oh, and if you've been to seventeen grocery stores and still can't find smoked mozzarella (because you are living in a global pandemic, for example) then it's totally cool to use smoked gouda instead.

HOT TIP ★ THE 9 × 13-INCH PAN YIELDS A THINNER PRODUCT BUT OPTIMIZES SURFACE AREA FOR MORE GOOEY CHEESE ON TOP. IF YOU WANT A DEEPER DISH, ASSEMBLE AND BAKE THIS IN AN 8 × 8-INCH PAN.

½ cup extra-virgin olive oil

2 medium eggplants (about 2 pounds total), peeled and cut into 1-inch chunks

Kosher salt

1 medium yellow or white onion, roughly chopped

8 garlic cloves, roughly chopped

2 teaspoons red pepper flakes

1 (14-ounce) can crushed tomatoes

2 tablespoons chopped fresh oregano

1 cup grated parmesan cheese

1 cup (3 ounces) low-moisture smoked mozzarella cheese, shredded

½ cup shredded low-moisture mozzarella cheese

2½ cups cooked quinoa, seasoned with salt

Chopped fresh Italian parsley, for serving

1. Preheat the oven to 375°F.

2. In a large Dutch oven, heat the olive oil over medium heat. When the oil shimmers, add the eggplant and salt and cook, stirring often, until the eggplant is soft, about 15 minutes.

3. Add the onion, garlic, and pepper flakes and cook for 5 minutes more. Add the tomatoes, one can's-worth of water, and the oregano. Stir to combine. Bring to a simmer, then reduce the heat to low, cover, and cook, stirring occasionally, until the sauce has cooked down and infused with flavor, about 30 minutes. Taste and season with salt as needed.

4. In a small bowl, combine the parmesan, smoked mozzarella, and mozzarella. Spread about 2 cups of the eggplant sauce in the bottom of a 9 × 13-inch baking dish. Spread half of the quinoa on top of the sauce, then top with about ¾ cup of the cheese blend. Repeat once, then add the remaining eggplant sauce and finish with the remaining cheese.

5. Bake until the sauce starts to bubble and the cheese is browned, about 30 minutes. Remove from the oven and let it cool for 10 minutes. Top with the parsley to serve.

Your hard work has added up to the best achievement of all: the ability to reach out and help others. The community you have helped build is truly supportive of the needs and dreams of all; you are free to begin again. Whatever seed you end up planting, your neighbors are there to pitch in, ensuring health, strength, and growth, just as you've done for them.

Nothing says abundance quite like a giant sandwich. Make this muffuletta as an offering to your collective before you venture back out on your own. There is just as much magick to go around as there is sandwich. Olive, oregano, and thyme will bring the whole group into loving, harmonious balance and ready you for the journey ahead.

MAGICKAL INGREDIENTS: OLIVE, OREGANO, THYME, BLACK PEPPER

VEGGIE MUFFULETTA

MAIN —— SERVES 6

The muffuletta originated in New Orleans, Louisiana. It's typically made with a large, round sesame loaf, layered with a mixture of olives, salami, ham, mortadella, Swiss, and provolone cheese, then sliced into wedges and served.

This is a *very* loose take on that sandwich. Feel free to make your own loose take on this recipe! The olive mixture needs to stay for it to be anything closely resembling a muffuletta, but you can use the rest of the ingredients listed as suggestions and add or omit any vegetables of your choice. If tomatoes aren't looking good, use zucchini, eggplant, or squash (be sure to cook them first). If you want to add some salami or a different kind of cheese, go for it. Be wary of adding things that are very wet, though, like vinegars, because they will sog out the bread, which is a major bummer.

HOT TIP ★ USE THE SLOW-ROASTED OLIVES (PAGE 153) IN LIEU OF WHOLE PITTED GREEN OLIVES TO MAKE THE OLIVE SPREAD.

1 crusty French boule (8- to 10-inch-diameter)
¼ cup extra-virgin olive oil
1 cup whole pitted green olives
¾ cup giardiniera
¼ cup sliced pepperoncini
½ pound fresh mozzarella cheese, sliced into ¼-inch rounds
Kosher salt and freshly ground black pepper
½ small red onion, thinly sliced
2 Persian (mini) cucumbers, thinly sliced
1 large tomato, sliced

2 teaspoons chopped fresh oregano or thyme

1. Preheat the oven to 450°F.

2. Halve the bread horizontally and scoop out some of the bread from the insides to make a small cavity to hold everything. Brush the olive oil on the cut sides of the bread and place on a baking sheet, cut-side up. Toast the bread until golden brown, 3 to 4 minutes.

3. In food processor, combine the olives, giardiniera, and pepperoncini and pulse until coarsely chopped.

4. Spread half the olive mixture on the bottom half the bread, then add the mozzarella and season with salt and pepper. Top with the onion, cucumbers, and tomato. Sprinkle with the oregano and add the remaining olive mixture. Place the other half of the bread on top and firmly press down. Wrap the sandwich in plastic wrap and put a weight on top to press it down. (A cast-iron pan with a large can of tomatoes sitting in it works great.) Let sit for about 30 minutes, then slice into wedges to serve.

PAGE OF COINS

EARTH OF EARTH ★ GROUNDING IN GROWTH

Get your hands in the dirt. Pull every last root previously planted here to get a fresh start on your garden. What you grew in the past has no bearing on what you plant now, so allow yourself to play with all possibilities before deciding on any one thing. It's rare to get to experiment so freely in the practical areas of life, so dig in and enjoy.

There are some places you just can't get to without trying things that seem crazy. This dessert is one of them. Caramel corn and grits aren't traditionally thought of as bosom buddies, yet here they are, all mixed up into one bowl of greatness. Topped with strawberries, symbols of Norse love and fertility goddess Freyja, it's got the power to keep your garden thriving.

MAGICKAL INGREDIENT: STRAWBERRIES

CARAMEL CORN GRITS
WITH FRESH STRAWBERRIES

DESSERT —— SERVES 6

This recipe turns traditional, creamy Southern grits into an earthy dessert reminiscent of caramel popcorn. Instead of cooking the grits in boring old regular water, we use *caramel water*. The result is a caramelized bowl of Southern hospitality (in corn form).

When buying the cornmeal, go for medium grind. (Fine grind also works, just don't use the quick-cooking kind.) If the grits get very thick or start to set up before they are cooked through, simply add more water to the pot to thin them out. You'll know when they are done because the grains will be very soft, and the consistency will be like a thick porridge. Take a little out and taste it. Does it taste cooked, delicious, caramelly, and corny? Then it's done!

HOT TIP ★ IF STRAWBERRIES ARE IN SEASON AND YOU HAVE ACCESS TO A FARMERS' MARKET, IT'LL MAKE A HUGE DIFFERENCE IF YOU BUY THEM THERE. LOOK FOR STRAWBERRIES THAT ARE SMALL IN SIZE AND DEEP RED; THEY TEND TO PACK THE MOST FLAVOR.

STRAWBERRIES

½ pint strawberries, hulled and quartered

3 tablespoons sugar

GRITS

1 cup sugar

¾ cup medium grind cornmeal

1 teaspoon kosher salt

4 tablespoons (2 ounces) unsalted butter

¼ cup heavy cream, plus more for drizzling

1 cup caramel popcorn, such as Popcornopolis

1. **MAKE THE STRAWBERRIES:** In a medium bowl, toss the strawberries with the sugar and let macerate at room temperature while you make the grits.

2. **MAKE THE GRITS:** Add ½ cup of the sugar to a medium saucepan and cook over medium heat, stirring often with a heatproof spatula until all the sugar has melted, about 3 minutes. Reduce the heat to low and cook, stirring constantly, until it foams up and turns dark brown and caramelized, 1 to 2 minutes longer.

3. Slowly add 4 cups water to the pot. The caramel will puff up, bubble, and release a lot of steam, then seize up. Increase the heat to medium and whisk until the caramel has dissolved again, then whisk in the cornmeal and salt. Increase the heat to high and bring the mixture to a boil, whisking constantly, until the cornmeal thickens and bubbles.

HOT TIP ★ WHEN YOU ADD THE WATER TO THE CARAMEL, DO SO VERY CAREFULLY—IT WILL SPUTTER AND STEAM UP AND TRY TO GIVE YOU A STEAM BURN. DON'T LET IT.

4. Reduce the heat to medium-low and cook, stirring frequently with a spatula, until thick and pulling away from the sides, about 50 minutes. If the grits become too thick before they are fully cooked through, add up to 1 cup water as needed.

5. Remove the pot from the heat and stir in the butter, cream, and remaining ½ cup sugar until combined.

6. Divide the grits evenly among the bowls. Top each with strawberries, caramel corn, and a drizzle of cream to serve.

KNIGHT OF COINS
FIRE OF EARTH ★ PASSIONATE CULTIVATION

The clay you've been kneading is taking form in your hands. You are preparing to send a creation of yours out into the world. The care you put into crafting it now will be your calling card in the future, so prioritize quality over quickness. Your ambition may get frustrated but will be better served in the end.

Patience is a great partner in making this brown sugar baked brioche. You can't rush it, but you can enjoy the process. If you feel like you need to be doing more, decide on an intention and knead it into the dough with every push of your hands. Look at you! You made a magick spell of your very own.

MAGICKAL INGREDIENT: SALT

BROWN SUGAR BAKED BRIOCHE

DESSERT —— SERVES 6

This recipe is for those who don't love overly sweet desserts. (It also makes a great breakfast.) During the baking process, you'll remove the brioche from the oven two times to poke lots of holes in it and "baste" it with heavy cream and light brown sugar. The cream soaks down into the holes, bringing some of the sugar with it, while the remaining cream mixture caramelizes on top for a sugary, fluffy baked brioche that's reminiscent of a sticky bun.

When you press the dough into the pan, it's kind of like you are making focaccia. The cold, stiff dough might be a little difficult to handle at first, but it will loosen up as you work with it.

HOT TIP ★ EVERYONE'S OVEN IS DIFFERENT. USE THE BAKING TIMES AS GUIDES AND RELY ON YOUR SENSES TO TELL WHEN IT'S DONE.

1¾ cups all-purpose flour

2 teaspoons granulated sugar

1 teaspoon kosher salt

1⅛ teaspoons active dry yeast

⅔ cup whole milk

6 tablespoons (3 ounces) unsalted butter, at room temperature

½ cup packed light brown sugar

½ cup heavy cream

1. In a stand mixer fitted with the hook, combine the flour, granulated sugar, salt, and yeast. Set the speed to low and slowly pour in the milk. Continue mixing on low until a shaggy dough forms, about 2 minutes, scraping the sides as needed.

2. Increase the speed to medium and continue mixing until a smooth, elastic dough forms, about 5 minutes.

3. Add the butter 1 tablespoon at a time, letting each fully incorporate before adding the next. Once all the butter is incorporated, mix on medium for about 5 minutes more, until the dough is smooth and elastic once again. Transfer the dough to a large greased bowl, cover tightly with plastic wrap, and let rise in the fridge overnight.

4. Grease a 9 × 13-inch sheet pan. Turn the dough out onto the pan and use your fingers to stretch the dough to fill the pan. Cover the dough with a kitchen towel and let it rise until it has doubled in size, about 2 hours, depending on the temperature of the room.

5. Preheat the oven to 375°F.

6. Bake the bread until a crust just starts to form, but the dough is still pale, about 10 minutes. Remove the pan from the oven and use a fork to poke holes all over. Really get in there, covering the top with dozens of tears and holes. (The bread should look a little bit like Freddy Krueger's face when you are done with it.) Sprinkle ¼ cup of the brown sugar evenly over the top. Drizzle with ¼ cup of the cream and spread it out evenly using the back of a spoon.

7. Return the bread to the oven and bake until the top and edges just start to brown, 15 to 20 minutes. Remove the bread from the oven and increase the oven temperature to 425°F. Use a fork to poke holes all over, sprinkle the remaining ¼ cup brown sugar on top and drizzle with the remaining ¼ cup cream. Return the bread to the oven and bake until the top is caramelized, 5 to 10 minutes more.

8. Let the bread cool for a few minutes. Slice and serve warm.

The foundation you are building will support your emotional and physical needs as well as those of your community. Don't worry about lack of resources. Anything you need can be obtained by planting the seeds in the ground you have made fertile with your careful tending. Stay true to your heart and everything you touch will grow heavy with fruit. Send down roots and drink in the bounty of the Earth.

An aspirational character in terms of prolific creation of life is the blackberry bush. They grow almost everywhere, so well that people freak out about them taking over their gardens. They provide sweet, delicious berries and they're not afraid to get a little mean to protect them.

MAGICKAL INGREDIENTS: BLACKBERRY, LEMON

BABY DUTCH BABIES

WITH BLACKBERRY BUTTER

DESSERT —— MAKES 12 DUTCH BABIES

A Dutch baby is a puffy cross between a crepe and a pancake—it's a sweet that falls on the slightly savory side of the spectrum. It's usually made as one giant baby, but this recipe uses a muffin tin to make 12 *baby* Dutch babies. You'll slather each one with blackberry butter right when they come out of the oven, adding a bright purple, tangy sweetness as it melts. Start to finish, this whole recipe comes together in about 30 minutes, making it great for eating morning, noon, or night.

The butter is heavy on the blackberries, so if yours are extra ripe and juicy, the butter may have a hard time staying emulsified. When you're done, it should be a vibrant deep-blue color and just barely holding together. If it breaks, you can either decide to be okay with that, or add a little bit more softened butter, 1 teaspoon at a time, until it holds together.

BLACKBERRY BUTTER

6 blackberries

2 tablespoons granulated sugar

¼ teaspoon kosher salt

4 tablespoons (2 ounces) unsalted butter, at room temperature

DUTCH BABIES

½ cup all-purpose flour

½ cup whole milk

3 large eggs

2 tablespoons granulated sugar

¼ teaspoon kosher salt

2 tablespoons unsalted butter, for the muffin tin

1 lemon, cut into wedges, for squeezing

Fresh blackberries, for garnish

Powdered sugar, for serving

1. Preheat the oven to 475°F. Place a 12-cup muffin tin inside to warm.

2. **MAKE THE BLACKBERRY BUTTER:** In a medium bowl, combine the blackberries, granulated sugar, and salt and mash them with a wooden spoon until the blackberries have broken down and released their juices. Add the butter and whisk vigorously to combine.

3. **MAKE THE DUTCH BABIES:** In a blender, combine the flour, milk, eggs, granulated sugar, and salt and blend until smooth, scraping down the sides as needed.

4. Remove the muffin tin from the oven and evenly coat each cup with the butter. Divide the batter evenly among the muffin cups (about 3 tablespoons per cup).

5. Bake until the Dutch babies are golden brown and have puffed up in the middle, about 15 minutes.

6. Immediately transfer the Dutch babies to a platter and top each one with a generous dollop of the blackberry butter and dust them with powdered sugar. Serve them hot with lemon wedges and fresh blackberries.

AIR OF EARTH ★ PLANNING FOR PLENTY

Clarity of mind is rushing through you now, helping you envision a strategy that ensures you are provided for. No more fighting for scraps, no more compromises or trading long-term prosperity for temporary security. Your life is in your hands now. Get the blueprints for your dream world in order and start building.

Together, prosperity and mental focus are unstoppable when constructing a sustainable system of growth. Pecans hold the power of both. They are a common addition to spells for money-drawing and luck. They are also associated with the element of Air, the wind beneath the wings of the suit of Swords and all the Kings. You get to receive their influence in the form of these buttered pecan sandie biscuits.

MAGICKAL INGREDIENT: PECANS

BUTTERED PECAN SANDIE BISCUITS

DESSERT —— MAKES 12 BISCUITS

These are not quite biscuits, yet not cookies either. They are kind of like pecan sandies, but softer and fluffier. Eat them at the end of a long day with a side of whiskey on the rocks.

These 12 sandie biscuits are pretty big. You could easily halve or double this recipe depending on how many people you want to feed. The best part about them is they last way longer than you think they should and will dry out and become more like pecan sandies with time. Keep them stored in an airtight container and they'll love you forever.

1 stick (4 ounces) unsalted butter

1 cup pecan pieces

1¾ cups all-purpose flour

½ cup granulated sugar

½ cup packed light brown sugar

2 teaspoons kosher salt

1½ teaspoons baking powder

¼ cup plus 2 tablespoons all-vegetable shortening, such as Spectrum

1 large egg

¼ cup heavy cream

1. In a large nonstick skillet, melt the butter over medium heat. Add the pecans and cook, stirring often, until they are golden brown and fragrant, about 3 minutes. Transfer the pecans and excess butter to a medium bowl and place in the fridge to cool.

2. In a large bowl, combine the flour, granulated sugar, brown sugar, salt, and baking powder. Add the shortening and cut it into the dough with your hands until it is sandy with pea-size lumps. Add the cooled pecan/butter mixture and combine, cutting any large bits of the butter into the dough. Stir in the egg and heavy cream until just combined.

3. Grease a baking sheet and line with parchment paper.

4. Scoop the batter into 12 even balls and place on the prepared baking sheet. Refrigerate for at least 30 minutes to chill.

5. Preheat the oven to 350°F.

6. Bake until the edges are golden brown, about 25 minutes, rotating the pan front to back halfway through. Let cool on the pan for 15 minutes.

MAJOR ARCANA

CENTERING MAGICKAL INGREDIENTS

Each card of the Major Arcana represents a piece of universal Divine wisdom. For home cooks, tarot wisdom can be awakened through the use of magickal ingredients—so we've homed in on some of our favorites based on Melinda's personal experience with ritual and spellwork. For the Major Arcana, we've paired one magickal ingredient with each of the twenty-two cards. Some of these ingredients have been used for the purposes we describe here for hundreds of years while others are more contemporary interpretations chosen based on Melinda's work.

The cards of the Major Arcana are what set the Tarot apart from any other deck of cards. While each of the suits of the Minor Arcana is associated with the earthly elements of Air, Fire, Water, and Earth, the Major Arcana cards are associated with the fifth element of Spirit. As you read through these recipes, some of these tarot archetypes will feel familiar (The Magician, The Moon) and some may seem a little more out there (The Hierophant, Temperance). Rest assured, every card here represents a figure or idea that played a major role in folklore in medieval Europe and long, long before and beyond. These archetypes are an inherent part of our collective humanity.

We invite you to view these figures not as some faraway, long-ago beings, but as parts of yourself. While the Minor Arcana generally speaks of **what we do,** the Major Arcana speaks of **who we are.** When you invite The Emperor to lead the way, for example, you are asking for a boost in your leadership skills and your ability to plan and execute large projects. When The Sun shows up to shine in your life, your perception will be sharpened and your eye naturally trained to find areas of your life most ripe for growth. Even cards often seen as scary have valuable wisdom to offer. We're here to help you drink it in . . . literally!

With these recipes, which run the gamut from cocktails and sides to desserts, mains, and everything in between, we hope to open you up to the endless ways you can use these magickal ingredients in cooking. To give you some signposts along the way, we've included the number of the card, the title, a mantra to give a little bite-size guidance, the magickal ingredient, and the purpose it serves. We encourage you to explore, to improvise, to awaken The Fool within and step boldly and joyfully into the unknown.

THE FOOL

ENJOY THE MOMENT, TRUST IN THE UNIVERSE.

Magickal Ingredient: Bergamot
Lifts the mood and relieves tension

Trusting, curious, and free from worry for the future or regret about the past, The Fool teaches us the value of presence and radical acceptance. When you follow The Fool, who you are, where you are, and what you are doing are all in perfect alignment with your higher purpose. What may look like naiveté is actually high wisdom. To experience this with a clear mind requires moving away from stress and toward joy— and bergamot is here to help!

The mood-lifting and tension-relieving properties of bergamot clear the way for deep appreciation of the present. Earl Grey tea carries the central magickal ingredient, while honey and lemon bring additional calm and clarity for maximum Fool integration.

ADDITIONAL MAGICKAL INGREDIENTS: HONEY, LEMON, ORANGE, ONION (SEE ALLIUMS)

BERGAMOT BAKED RICE
WITH CITRUS AND HONEY

SIDE —— SERVES 4

This is anything but a simple baked rice dish. Well, actually, it's really simple to make, but that's where it ends. As the rice cooks, it soaks up the Earl Grey tea that it's bathing in, giving it earthiness and depth. When you add that to the salty-sweet notes of caramelized onions, some honey, and a zing of citrus, well, you'd be a *fool* to skip this recipe. If you are lucky enough to have leftovers, try frying up the rice with an egg and some soy sauce for a delicious take on fried rice.

2 bags Earl Grey tea
1 lemon
1 blood orange
4 tablespoons (2 ounces) unsalted butter
1 tablespoon extra-virgin olive oil
1 medium yellow onion, diced
Kosher salt
4 tablespoons honey
1 cup basmati rice

1. Preheat the oven to 425°F.

2. Bring 1¾ cups water to a boil in a small saucepan. Once boiling, add the tea bags and remove the saucepan from the heat.

3. Meanwhile, grate the zest from the lemon and blood orange and set the zest aside. Halve the lemon and squeeze the juice from one half. Cut the other half into ¼-inch-thick rounds. Cut the orange into ¼-inch-thick rounds.

4. In a large skillet, heat the butter and olive oil over medium-low heat. When the butter has melted, add the onion and sauté, stirring occasionally, until soft and lightly browned, about 15 minutes. Taste and add salt as needed. Add 2 tablespoons of the honey, the lemon zest, and blood orange zest and cook until the onions are caramelized, about 10 minutes more.

5. Transfer the onions to a 2-quart baking dish and spread in an even layer. Top the onions with the rice in an even layer, and sprinkle with 1 teaspoon kosher salt. Arrange as many of the lemon and blood orange rounds as you can fit in an even layer on top.

6. Remove the tea bags from the saucepan, squeezing out as much flavorful liquid as you can. Return the saucepan to the heat and bring the tea to a boil over high heat. Once boiling, remove the pan from heat and pour evenly over the contents of the baking dish.

7. Cover the dish tightly with foil, transfer to the oven, and bake until the water has been absorbed and the rice is fluffy and lightly browned around the edges, about for 30 minutes.

8. Remove from the oven, uncover, and remove the lemon and blood orange rounds to use as a garnish, Drizzle with the lemon juice and the remaining 2 tablespoons honey. Re-cover with the foil and let sit about 10 minutes. Fluff the rice and serve.

THE MAGICIAN

DREAM IT, CONJURE IT.

Magickal Ingredient: Cinnamon
Inspires self-mastery through connection with the Universe

You are the creator of your world. No matter your circumstances or resources, you have the ability to change your personal domain. Your power is an extension of the connection you have with the Earth and the Universe, these celestial bodies that all ultimately came from the same place as you. Call on these siblings when you need assistance aligning your experience with your ideals. Then, kick back with a glass of this Butterfly Pea Flower Cinnamon Gimlet and wait for the visions to come floating in.

Used as a magickal accelerator in many spells, cinnamon packs an energetic punch all on its own, activating your power as much as your taste buds. The stress-reducing properties of butterfly pea flower allow you to fully enjoy the awakening.

ADDITIONAL MAGICKAL INGREDIENTS: BUTTERFLY PEA FLOWER, LEMON

BUTTERFLY PEA FLOWER CINNAMON GIMLET

COCKTAIL —— MAKES 1 COCKTAIL

A classic gimlet is two parts gin, one part lime, and some simple syrup for good measure, shaken and served up. This is not a classic gimlet—it's full of magick—and even though true magicians should never reveal their tricks, we're gonna have to. Wait to add the lemon juice until after you serve it. The butterfly pea flower syrup reacts with the acidity and changes from electric blue to deep purple for a swirling tie-dye effect. Just serve the cocktail with the lemon on the rim of the glass and tell your friends to squeeze the juice and drop the rind into their drinks to watch the magick unfold!

HOT TIP ★ FOR A NONALCOHOLIC VERSION OF THIS DRINK, ADD 2 OUNCES BUTTERFLY PEA SYRUP TO AN 8-OUNCE GLASS, ADD ICE, AND TOP WITH CLUB SODA. DON'T FORGET TO SQUEEZE IN A WEDGE OF LEMON OR LIME TO CREATE THE MAGICK EFFECT.

2½ ounces gin
½ ounce Butterfly Pea Syrup (recipe follows)
¼ lemon, for serving

1. In a cocktail shaker, combine the gin and pea flower syrup. Add ice. Shake well to combine, about 30 seconds. Strain into a coupe glass.

2. Position the lemon wedge on the rim of the glass and give instructions to the recipient for squeezing in the lemon juice before drinking.

BUTTERFLY PEA SYRUP

MAKES ABOUT ¾ CUP

2 cinnamon sticks
1 tablespoon whole dried butterfly pea flowers
½ cup sugar

1. In a small saucepan, combine ½ cup water, the cinnamon sticks, and butterfly pea flowers and bring to a boil over medium-high heat. Once boiling, remove the pot from the heat and let steep for about 10 minutes, or until bright blue. Strain the liquid into a small bowl and discard the cinnamon sticks and pea flowers.

2. Return the liquid to the saucepan and stir in the sugar. Bring to a boil over medium-high heat. Remove from the heat and stir to make sure all the sugar has dissolved. Let cool to room temperature, then refrigerate to chill before using. Store in an airtight container in the fridge for up to 1 month.

THE HIGH PRIESTESS

CREATE A SANCTUARY, TRAVEL INWARD.

Magickal Ingredient: Pomegranate
Promotes facing fears to gather wisdom

Secure within the boundaries she has set, The High Priestess devotes herself completely to cultivating respect for the teachings of the Universe. When we align ourselves with this energy, we begin to carve out space for cleansing, connection, and reflection. Sometimes it seems impossible to find time to honor and learn from the world around us. Take a cue from The High Priestess and prioritize the creation of a space to receive sacred knowledge.

Pomegranate has long been regarded as a holy fruit and symbol of abundance. Here, we use it to open the door to sacred teachings of the ages. As a bonus, mint keeps the vibes high and opens up your perception beyond the five senses, ensuring maximum absorption of all that wisdom.

ADDITIONAL MAGICKAL INGREDIENT: MINT

POMEGRANATE JULEP

COCKTAIL —— MAKES 1 COCKTAIL

A mint julep is made with bourbon, mint, and simple syrup and is often sipped at the Kentucky Derby. This twist on the classic uses pomegranate juice to brighten it and also give it a beautiful pink hue. To make fresh pomegranate juice, simply add a few spoonfuls of seeds at a time to a lemon squeezer and squeeze! Be careful, though, because the juice will squirt out from the sides and make a mess. A FUN mess, but a mess, nonetheless. Alternatively, you can buy pomegranates already juiced at the grocery store.

Serve this drink the traditional way over crushed ice and with a mint sprig garnish and if you don't have a julep cup or mule mug, feel free to use a 12-ounce tumbler.

10 large fresh mint leaves, plus more for garnish
½ ounce Simple Syrup (recipe follows)
2 ounces bourbon
1 ounce pomegranate juice

1. In a julep cup or mule mug, use a muddler or a wooden spoon to gently mash the mint leaves and simple syrup until fragrant. Stir in the bourbon and pomegranate juice, then add crushed ice until full.

2. Give it one more stir to combine, garnish with a sprig of mint, and get ready for the races.

HOT TIP ★ MUDDLING IS A BAR TERM THAT MEANS TO GENTLY MASH AND MASSAGE. USE A WOODEN MUDDLER TO ACHIEVE THIS EFFECT AND RELEASE THE FLAVOR OF WHATEVER IT IS THAT YOU'RE MUDDLING.

SIMPLE SYRUP

MAKES ABOUT ¾ CUP

½ cup sugar

1. In a small saucepan, combine the sugar and ½ cup water and bring to a boil over medium-high heat to dissolve the sugar. Remove from the heat and let cool.

2. Transfer to an airtight container and store in the fridge for up to 1 month.

THE EMPRESS

LOVE FREELY, WELCOME ABUNDANCE.

Magickal Ingredient: Rose

Amplifies love, given and received

You know that feeling that fills you up and makes you believe you can do anything? That feeling that grows from a smile or a hug or words of encouragement? That is The Empress shining love into your life. When we embody Empress energy, we focus the beam of our heart on what we want to increase in our lives and watch as a beautiful garden of abundance blossoms around us. Open your heart, make yourself vulnerable, and you can receive just as much love as you give.

This simple rose water spritz is a perfect companion to an afternoon in the garden. Rose opens the heart and increases the flow of love. When love increases, fear decreases, and we are free to pour that love energy into anything we want to grow.

ADDITIONAL MAGICKAL INGREDIENT: ELDERFLOWER

A ROSE IS A ROSE IS A ROSÉ PUNCH

COCKTAIL —— SERVES 12

Gertrude Stein once wrote, "A rose is a rose is a rose is a rose," and she was right—but when you add a bottle of rosé, some rose water, and rose petal ice cubes, you transform the rose into a drinkable punch and it goes down *real* easy. Rose water can be overpowering, so start with just 1 tablespoon and add 1 teaspoon at a time for a stronger flavor.

This punch gets extra rose-power from its ice cubes, each one encasing a few dainty petals. Be sure to make them a couple days in advance. Fill a jumbo ice cube tray with water and add a couple rose petals or a rosebud to each before freezing. The petals will float to the top and freeze there, partially submerged, and when you use them in the punch, you'll smell them with every sip. Repeat this process until you have at least 12 large cubes stockpiled.

HOT TIP ★ FOR PARTIES, SERVE THE PUNCH OUT OF A PUNCH BOWL SET ON A TABLE COVERED IN ROSE PETALS. PLACE TUMBLERS, AN ICE BUCKET FILLED WITH THE PETAL CUBES, AND THE CLUB SODA ON THE SIDE. DRINKERS CAN ADD THE PUNCH AND THE ICE TO THEIR OWN GLASSES AND TOP EACH OFF WITH THE CLUB SODA.

1 (750 ml) bottle rosé wine

1½ cups elderflower liqueur

1 tablespoon rose water

1 liter club soda, for topping

1. In a large pitcher or punch bowl, combine the rosé wine, elderflower liqueur, and rose water. Chill in the refrigerator until ready to serve.

2. Fill glasses with ice and pour in the punch. Top with club soda to serve.

HOT TIP ★ TO MAKE PUNCH FOR ONE, FOLLOW THE SAME PROCESS WITH THESE MEASUREMENTS: 2 OUNCES ROSÉ, 1 OUNCE ELDERFLOWER LIQUEUR, AND ¼ TEASPOON ROSE WATER. ADD ICE AND TOP IT OFF WITH CLUB SODA.

THE EMPEROR

IV

MAKE A PLAN, MAKE A KINGDOM.

Magickal Ingredient: Cayenne pepper
Ignites motivation and courage

When your vision clears and the road ahead becomes evident, when you feel like you could move mountains but you'd rather delegate, when your objective is so compelling you're inspired just thinking about it—you've got that Emperor feeling. This is strong-willed and straight-shooting energy. Though The Emperor sometimes gets a bad reputation for being sharp and forceful, those edges can easily be softened with awareness and compassion. Don't be afraid to call on this power to accomplish greatness. Celebrate your decision and fire it up with our michelada.

Cayenne offers the intensity of The Emperor while the brightness of lime brings some extra inspiration. Fix yourself a classic michelada in a glass rimmed with a Tajín-cayenne salt, kick back, and plan out your empire.

ADDITIONAL MAGICKAL INGREDIENT: LIME

CLASSIC MICHELADA
WITH TAJÍN-CAYENNE SALT

COCKTAIL —— SERVES 2

Nothing beats a michelada on a Sunday afternoon and this version is classic—because why mess with perfection? You can use whatever hot sauce you like, but Crystal brand specifically uses cayenne peppers, so if you want extra Emperor energy, go with that.

2 teaspoons Tajín clásico seasoning

Pinch of cayenne pepper

2 lime wedges

12 ounces Clamato

¼ cup fresh lime juice

1 tablespoon Worcestershire sauce

¾ teaspoon Maggi seasoning

2 teaspoons hot sauce, such as Crystal

2 (12-ounce) cans Mexican lager, such as Tecate

1. On a small plate, stir together the Tajín and cayenne. Rub the rims of 2 pint glasses with the lime wedges and dip the rims in the mixture to coat.

2. In a pitcher, combine the Clamato, lime juice, Worcestershire sauce, Maggi, and hot sauce. Fill the glasses with ice, pour in the Clamato mixture, and top each with a beer. Serve the remaining beer on the side.

HOT TIP ★ THE CLAMATO BASE FOR THE MICHELADAS CAN EASILY BE DOUBLED, TRIPLED, OR QUADRUPLED TO SUIT YOUR NEEDS AND ONCE MADE, WILL LAST FOR 1 MONTH. SIMPLY COMBINE ALL THE INGREDIENTS AND STORE THE BASE IN THE FRIDGE, THEN RIM THE GLASSES AND ADD THE BEERS WHENEVER THE OCCASION ARISES.

THE HIEROPHANT
LEARN FROM THE MASTERS, ELEVATE YOUR VIBE.

Magickal Ingredient: Frankincense
Encourages exploration of Divine teachings

You are not alone. Spiritual teachers throughout time stand ready to take your hand and guide you. Hierophants are the flame holders of spiritual traditions and their purpose is to pass their teachings on to keep them alive. When you invite this energy into your life, you not only open yourself to receive Divine teachings, you also enter into the understanding that when the time comes, you will pass them on to someone else in need.

For thousands of years, frankincense has been used medicinally and spiritually. This recipe brings its time-tested power into your life in a refreshing twist on the classic Pimm's Cup. The addition of lemon brings a little extra optimism and clarity to the party.

ADDITIONAL MAGICKAL INGREDIENTS: LEMON, MINT, ROSEMARY

FRANKINPIMM'S CUP

COCKTAIL —— MAKES 1 COCKTAIL

Pimm's is an English liqueur that lends itself to fruity, crisp flavors and it's perfect for light, easy drinking. In this twist on the classic, rosemary and cucumber are the star ingredients, playing off the spicy, woody citrus notes of frankincense like a charm. Word to the wise (this is The Hierophant card, after all): Frankincense is an extremely strong flavor, so start with just one drop of the oil and add more to taste, one drop at a time.

½ Persian (mini) cucumber, sliced into ½-inch rounds

1 drop frankincense essential oil, plus more to taste

3 ounces Pimm's No. 1

1 ounce gin (optional)

½ ounce fresh lemon juice

1 (6.8-ounce) bottle ginger beer, such as Fever Tree, for topping

1 large sprig mint, for serving

1 large sprig rosemary, for serving

1 lemon wedge, for serving

1. In a pint glass, use a muddler or a wooden spoon to gently mash the cucumber and frankincense until fragrant. Stir in the Pimm's, gin (if using), and lemon juice. Fill the glass with ice and top with the ginger beer. If desired, add more frankincense oil, one drop at a time, to taste.

2. Garnish with the mint, rosemary, and lemon wedge.

HOT TIP ★ SLAP THE MINT AND ROSEMARY BETWEEN YOUR PALMS BEFORE GARNISHING TO HELP RELEASE THE AROMA.

THE LOVERS

LOVE YOURSELF BEFORE LOVING ANOTHER.

Magickal Ingredient: Vanilla
Helps attract a suitable counterpart

This card could more accurately be called The Partners but The Lovers has such a great ring to it, doesn't it? To find lasting love and partnership—romantic or otherwise—we must identify our differences. This allows us to cherish the complementary skills we bring to a relationship and to identify places prone to conflict so we can address them early and often. Only when we see the contour of our own puzzle piece can we find another that fits just right.

Whether you are searching for a new love or wanting to strengthen the one you've got, vanilla will steer you in the right direction. Call on this energy when you are looking for a romantic partner, to fortify a friendship, or to pursue a business partnership.

ADDITIONAL MAGICKAL INGREDIENT: HONEY

VANILLA PANNA COTTA
WITH SHERRY GASTRIQUE

DESSERT —— SERVES 6

The trick to every panna cotta is adding the perfect amount of gelatin so that it holds together just barely enough to make it to your face, then melts in your mouth when you spoon it in. The trick to *this* panna cotta is the zing of the sherry vinegar, which counteracts the sweetness of the cream for an unparalleled taste sensation, once again proving that opposites do, indeed, attract.

HOT TIP ★ WHEN STIRRING, TRY TO INCORPORATE AS LITTLE AIR INTO THE MIXTURE AS POSSIBLE. THIS WILL MAKE FOR A DENSER, CREAMIER PANNA COTTA.

PANNA COTTA

3 sheets silver gelatin or 1 (0.25-ounce) envelope powdered gelatin

3 cups heavy cream

½ cup sugar

¼ teaspoon kosher salt

2 vanilla beans, split lengthwise, or 1 tablespoon pure vanilla extract

1 cup whole milk

GASTRIQUE

⅓ cup sherry vinegar

3 tablespoons honey

2 tablespoons sugar

Pinch of kosher salt

1. **MAKE THE PANNA COTTA:** Bloom the gelatin.

HOT TIP ★ TO BLOOM SHEET GELATIN, SUBMERGE IT IN A MEDIUM BOWL FILLED WITH ICE WATER UNTIL IT IS COMPLETELY SOFT, ABOUT 2 MINUTES. REMOVE THE GELATIN FROM THE BOWL, SQUEEZE OUT EXCESS WATER, AND SET ASIDE. TO BLOOM POWDERED GELATIN, SPRINKLE IT IN AN EVEN LAYER OVER 4 TABLESPOONS COLD WATER AND LET IT SOFTEN COMPLETELY IN THE WATER FOR 3 TO 5 MINUTES. SCOOP IT OUT BEFORE ADDING IT TO THE HOT LIQUID.

2. In a medium pot, combine 2 cups of the heavy cream, the sugar, and salt. Scrape the vanilla seeds into the pot (or add the vanilla extract if using) and bring to a simmer over medium heat. Once simmering, remove the pot from the heat and let the vanilla steep in the cream for 10 minutes to infuse. Remove the vanilla beans (if using). Return the mixture to medium heat and bring to a simmer. Remove from heat, add the bloomed gelatin, and gently stir until it completely dissolves into the cream.

3. Stir in the remaining 1 cup heavy cream and the milk until combined. Pour the mixture into an 8 × 8-inch baking dish and cover the top directly with plastic wrap to prevent a skin from forming. Refrigerate for 6 hours or up to overnight to set.

4. **MEANWHILE, MAKE THE GASTRIQUE:** In a small saucepan, combine the sherry vinegar, honey, sugar, and salt and bring to a simmer over medium-high heat. Reduce heat to low and cook, stirring often, until the mixture reduces to a syrup-like consistency, about 10 minutes. Remove from the heat and let cool to room temperature.

5. To serve, pour the gastrique over the panna cotta, using the back of a spoon or a spatula to spread it in a thin, even layer.

THE CHARIOT

HELP IS HERE, ALLOW IT TO CARRY YOU.

VII

Magickal Ingredient: Chicory
Clears the way for luck to arrive

You've put in the work. The ball is rolling. Progress is being made. The Chariot brings luck and wisdom: the luck of the right help arriving at the right time and the wisdom to know when to accept it. It can be hard to relinquish control and just ride along for a spell. Try not to worry. Your Chariot will come for you exactly when you need it, not to take away what you've created, but to capitalize on the momentum you've built.

When you want to call your Chariot in, chew on some chicory. The roots are sometimes dried, ground, and added to coffee, but we like the crunch of fresh chicory leaves between the teeth to really get our wheels turning—and what better match for a Chariot than a Caesar?

ADDITIONAL MAGICKAL INGREDIENTS: LEMON, HONEY, GARLIC (SEE ALLIUMS), BLACK PEPPER, MUSTARD

CHICORY CAESAR

SIDE —— SERVES 4 TO 6

Chicories are the hearty, bitter cousins of lettuce. The term is a catch-all for many varieties, including radicchio, endive, escarole, and frisée, and you can use any combination thereof for this salad. The bold, garlicky Caesar dressing blessed with a touch of honey balances the bitterness of the chicories; the toasty bread crumbs add the perfect crunch. They will get soggy if they sit in the salad for too long, so add them just before serving.

Use the 1-pound chicory measurement as a guide, but also use your eyes. Ultimately you want enough chicories to make 8 or 9 cups of loosely packed leaves. And for an extra-flavorful dressing, use the leftover olive oil from the Poached Tuna (page 89). It's a total baller move.

DRESSING

1 garlic clove, peeled

2 anchovy fillets

1 teaspoon kosher salt, plus more to taste

1 large egg yolk

2 teaspoons Dijon mustard

3 tablespoons fresh lemon juice

1 tablespoon honey

½ teaspoon hot sauce

3 tablespoons freshly grated parmesan cheese

¼ cup extra-virgin olive oil

Freshly ground black pepper

SALAD

1 tablespoon unsalted butter or extra-virgin olive oil

¼ cup plain dried bread crumbs

½ teaspoon sugar

Pinch of kosher salt

1 pound chicories, washed and roughly chopped or torn

Freshly grated parmesan cheese, for serving

1. **MAKE THE DRESSING:** In a mortar and pestle or food processor, combine the garlic, anchovies, and salt and mash/process until a paste forms.

2. In a medium bowl, whisk together the anchovy paste, egg yolk, mustard, lemon juice, honey, hot sauce, and parmesan until fully combined. Slowly add the olive oil while whisking constantly until thickened and emulsified. Taste and season with salt and pepper as needed. Store the dressing in an airtight container in the fridge up to 4 days.

3. **MAKE THE SALAD:** In a medium skillet, melt the butter over medium heat. Add the bread crumbs and toast them for 1 minute, stirring often. Add the sugar and salt and continue cooking, stirring constantly, until the bread crumbs are lightly browned, about 1 more minute. Remove the skillet from heat and transfer the bread crumbs to a plate to cool.

4. Add the chicories and dressing to a large bowl and toss until coated. Let sit for 5 minutes, then add the bread crumbs and combine. Top with parmesan and serve immediately.

STRENGTH

TRUE STRENGTH IS FELT, NOT SHOWN.

Magickal Ingredient: Ginger
Supports courage and trusting instincts

The Strength card offers the wisdom of confident restraint. To be full of life force and vitality, yet still. While we often think of strength in terms of physicality, there's so much more to it than muscle. We are at our strongest when we are emotionally vulnerable and impervious to provocation. Strength means conserving your energy for what you want to fight *for*, not against.

The heat in ginger that makes it useful for opening sinuses also works for opening your heart and trusting in your own power. It has been used medicinally for thousands of years and is a common ingredient to add the energy of Elemental Fire to spells. Whip up these slushies when you need a little courage—the vodka won't hurt your cause.

ADDITIONAL MAGICKAL INGREDIENTS: LIME, MINT

MOSCOW MULE MELON SLUSHIES

COCKTAIL —— SERVES 4

This is a cocktail and a snack all rolled into one, and it's the perfect way to while away a late-summer afternoon. The addition of ginger adds a strong bite of spice that balances out the sweetness of the melon and the acidity of the lime juice.

Cantaloupe and honeydew are great, but if you have access to a farmers' market, go check out which heirloom varieties are available. You'd be surprised at how deep the melon world gets.

½ small (3- to 4-pound) cantaloupe or honeydew melon, seeded and rind removed
½ cup vodka
2 tablespoons fresh lime juice
⅓ cup Ginger Syrup (recipe follows)
2 cups ginger beer
4 sprigs mint, for serving

1. Cut the melon into chunks and add it to a blender. Add the vodka, lime juice, and ginger syrup and blend on high until the melon is pureed.

2. Stir in the ginger beer and pour the mixture into a double-lined 1-gallon zip-top bag. Place it in the freezer for at least 8 hours.

3. Remove the bag from the freezer and break up any large chunks of ice by squeezing the bag. Divide the mixture among 4 frosty glasses and garnish each slushy with a mint sprig. Serve with a spoon and a straw.

GINGER SYRUP

MAKES ½ CUP

2 inches fresh ginger, sliced
⅓ cup sugar

1. In a small saucepan, combine the ginger, sugar. and ⅓ cup water. Bring to a boil over medium-high heat. Remove from the heat, stir to combine, and let steep for 1 hour.

2. Strain the syrup through a fine-mesh sieve and let cool completely.

THE HERMIT

SPEND TIME ALONE, GATHERING WISDOM.

Magickal Ingredient: Licorice Root
Provides shelter needed to integrate information

Not simply a recluse who shuns the company of others, The Hermit is a figure that invites us to take on intentional solitude. Set aside a good chunk of time, turn off your screens, and think about what you want to do when you give yourself this space. How do you want to expand? What do you want to offer others when you emerge from your cocoon? Your time and energy are valuable. Spend them on something you can be proud of.

To get the most out of your alone time, you need some protection from the outside world. Licorice is here to provide. Just as a tea made from this root lends a soothing shield to a sore throat, licorice used in any magick—including this homemade sauerkraut—can be called on to shield you from distractions so you can focus on your metamorphosis.

ADDITIONAL MAGICKAL INGREDIENT: CARAWAY SEEDS

SAUERKRAUT
FROM SCRATCH

SIDE —— MAKES ABOUT 1½ QUARTS

Sauerkraut is surprisingly easy to make. The only tricky part is it will be slightly different every time you do it. You'll leave it at room temperature to ferment and if the room is very hot, fermentation can happen in a matter of days. If it's quite cold, it could take up to 3 or 4 weeks. Ideally, it will be somewhere in between.

The most important thing is that the cabbage needs to stay submerged in its liquid. If it doesn't, there is an easy fix: Add more water! When doing so, add ½ teaspoon kosher salt for each ¼ cup water you add. If you happen to notice any weird scum forming on top of the kraut, scrape it off and discard it. The stuff underneath is pure gold.

Most sauerkraut recipes do not include licorice root, but the flavor lends itself subtly to the tangy kraut. Licorice root can be a real pain to cut. Instead, use your hands to break it up as best you can and aim for 1- to 2-inch chunks.

1 medium head green cabbage (about 3 pounds)
2 tablespoons kosher salt
1½ teaspoons caraway seeds
8-inch piece licorice root, broken into chunks

1. Remove the outermost cabbage leaf and set aside. Thinly slice the rest of the cabbage, add it to a large bowl with the salt, and toss to coat. Massage the cabbage until it begins to release water. Continue for about 10 minutes, until the released liquid fully covers the cabbage when pressed to the bottom. If more than 15 minutes of massaging have passed and the water doesn't submerge the cabbage, go on to the next step.

2. Add the caraway seeds and licorice root to the bowl and combine.

3. Transfer the cabbage to a 2-quart airtight container or canning jar. Press it to the bottom then pour over the liquid. If needed, add cold water until the cabbage is submerged (see headnote). Place the reserved cabbage leaf on top of the mixture and cover the mouth of the container with cheesecloth and a rubber band.

4. Place the container in a baking dish or sheet pan (something with a rim) and let sit at room temperature to ferment for anywhere between 4 days and 4 weeks (see headnote). Make sure the kraut is always covered with liquid. If necessary, tamp down the fermenting cabbage every couple of days to keep it submerged. When it starts to bubble, leave it out for up to 3 more days, until it tastes fermented and slightly effervescent, then cover and transfer to the fridge. Store it in an airtight container in the fridge for up to 1 month.

IF THE CABBAGE DOESN'T STAY SUBMERGED BY ITSELF, YOU MAY NEED TO WEIGHT IT DOWN. A SMALL PLATE WORKS FOR EXTRA-WIDE CONTAINERS. IF YOU ARE USING A WIDE-MOUTH JAR, FILL A SMALLER JAR WITH MARBLES AND PLACE THAT ON TOP.

WHEEL OF FORTUNE
EVERYTHING MOVES IN PERFECT TIME.
BE PATIENT AND BE READY.

Magickal Ingredient: Nutmeg
Facilitates inner expansion and growth

This card represents one of those classic good news/bad news situations, except both pieces of news are actually the same: The Universe wants you to embrace the pace of your growth. Whether you think life is moving too slowly or quickly, you're wrong. Full acceptance of the present is needed. But acceptance is not always comfortable. Personal development can hurt. This analgesic tiki cocktail is here to help.

    The nutmeg garnish in this fortune-filled cocktail carries powers of persuasion, pulling your perspective into a "good news" space when confronted with challenges. While your outer vision may get blurry, your inner vision will be kept clear and honest with the help of some coconut.

ADDITIONAL MAGICKAL INGREDIENT: COCONUT, LIME, ORANGE

SLAYER OF PAIN

COCKTAIL —— MAKES 1 COCKTAIL

The Painkiller, which is what this drink is based on, was invented by Daphne Henderson at the Soggy Dollar Bar in the British Virgin Islands in the 1970s and it has stood the test of time.

    Crushed ice is ideal but cubed will work if it's all you got. And be sure to use pineapple juice with no added sugar, otherwise this will be more of a dessert than a cocktail. Add a little tangerine or mandarin orange juice, plus a hint of lime, and this drink doesn't just kill pain, it slays it.

4 ounces pineapple juice

2 ounces dark rum

1 ounce freshly squeezed tangerine or mandarin orange

1 ounce sweetened cream of coconut, such as Coco Lopez

½ ounce freshly squeezed lime juice

Freshly grated nutmeg, for serving

¼-inch-thick orange wheel, for serving

1. In a cocktail shaker, combine the pineapple juice, rum, orange juice, coconut cream, lime juice, and ice. Shake vigorously for about 30 seconds, or until frothy. Fill a tiki mug or highball glass with crushed ice and strain the drink over it.

2. Top with freshly grated nutmeg on top and garnish with the orange "wheel of fortune."

XI

JUSTICE

ALLOW THE SCALES TO BALANCE, RETURN TO CENTER.

Magickal Ingredient: Olive
Offers the gift of peace and harmony

When the harmony is off in some area of your life, call on Justice to bring it back. This energy is a seesaw, there are no shortcuts to balancing it out. Sleeping too little? You'll likely need to sleep too much to return to center. Feeling chronically unappreciated? It's gonna take more than a few words of encouragement to set you right. While you begin pulling your energy toward a peaceful equilibrium, enjoy this little snack.

Olives and the branches they grow on have been considered symbols of peace for thousands of years. So, why reinvent the wheel? These slow-roasted olives bring in some bonus magick (garlic for protection, rosemary for heart healing, and lemon for positivity) to entice you to remain in a blissfully balanced state.

ADDITIONAL MAGICKAL INGREDIENTS: GARLIC (SEE ALLIUMS),
ROSEMARY, LEMON, THYME

SLOW-ROASTED OLIVES

SNACK —— SERVES 4 TO 6

What's more olive-y than olives slow-roasted in olive oil? Use whatever kind you like, with or without pits. Just be sure to let anyone eating know the pit-uation (more than one tooth has been lost this way).

Rosemary and thyme are a classic herb pairing for olives, but marjoram, oregano, or sage would be great, too—use whatever herbs you like. Feel free to add other things to the mix along with the garlic and lemon. Dried chiles would be a great addition. Or shallots. Basically, there is no wrong way to do this.

These are just as great for snacking as they are for making martinis *extra* dirty or as part of the Party Board (page 159). For bonus points, you can also use them in the Veggie Muffuletta (page 122). Or simply save the excess oil to use in salad dressings or to cook with.

3 cups assorted olives, drained

½ cup extra-virgin olive oil

6 garlic cloves, smashed and peeled

1 small lemon, sliced into ¼-inch-thick rounds

3 sprigs fresh rosemary

6 sprigs fresh thyme

1. Preheat the oven to 300°F.

2. In an 8 × 8-inch baking dish, combine the olives, olive oil, garlic, lemon rounds, rosemary, and thyme and toss to coat. Cover with foil and bake until fragrant and the lemons are soft, 2½ to 3 hours, stirring every 30 minutes.

3. Serve warm or at room temperature. Just be sure to declare, "JUSTICE IS SERVED" loudly and firmly whenever you do it.

THE HANGED MAN

SHIFT YOUR PERSPECTIVE TO CHANGE YOUR WORLD.

Magickal Ingredient: Mushrooms
Eases fear to encourage adventure

This card may seem morbid, but the wisdom it provides is anything but. The man in question invites you to join him in hanging upside down to change your perspective, widening your field of possibilities. You might notice things from this perspective you couldn't see before—about yourself and your place in the world. Not into literally hanging upside down? No problem. Anything you do to knock yourself out of your routine will do. Or, you can go straight to the delicious part and eat our mushroom panzanella.

   Mushrooms come in many varieties, some more . . . adventurous than others. While most have specific uses and associations, all are good for coaxing you out of your shell and running wild, so feel free to explore your options.

ADDITIONAL MAGICKAL INGREDIENTS: THYME, OREGANO, GARLIC (SEE ALLIUMS), MUSTARD, BLACK PEPPER, CHILE, PARSLEY, RED PEPPER FLAKES (SEE CHILES)

ROASTED MUSHROOMS
AND RYE PANZANELLA

SIDE —— SERVES 4 TO 6

The rye, mushrooms, and Comté cheese bring earthy depth to this dish, while the tomato vinaigrette keeps it light and breezy enough for a late summer/early fall salad. It's great to make in advance or for a picnic, but make sure the bread is well toasted or you will end up with a pile of mush. And the riper the tomatoes, the better it will be.

   Use any kind of mushroom you like. You can keep it simple with white button mushrooms or get real fancy with a mix of morels and chanterelles. We like to use an assortment of whatever looks best from the market. Roasting time varies according to the size and type of mushrooms—just be sure to roast them until they are extra browned and crisp on the edges for the tastiest results.

HOT TIP ★ COMTÉ CAN BE SWAPPED OUT FOR ANY MILD, MEDIUM-FIRM CHEESE, LIKE GRUYÈRE OR FONTINA.

5 cups stale rye bread, cut or torn into 1-inch chunks

9 tablespoons extra-virgin olive oil

¾ pound assorted mushrooms, halved or cut into 1-inch chunks if they are very large

1 teaspoon red pepper flakes (optional)

Kosher salt and freshly ground black pepper

3 tablespoons sherry vinegar

1 tablespoon chopped fresh thyme or oregano

1 teaspoon Dijon mustard

½ teaspoon minced garlic

1 extra-large tomato, roughly chopped

½ cup grated Comté cheese, plus more for topping

¼ cup roughly chopped fresh Italian parsley

1. Preheat the oven to 400°F.

2. Add the bread and 2 tablespoons of the olive oil to a sheet pan and toss to coat. Spread them out in an even layer and bake until dry and browned, 10 to 12 minutes. Remove them from the oven and let cool for 5 minutes. Transfer to a large bowl. Leave the oven on and hold on to the sheet pan.

3. In a medium bowl, combine the mushrooms, pepper flakes, 3 tablespoons of the olive oil, and salt and pepper to taste and toss to coat. Spread the mushrooms in an even layer on the reserved sheet pan and bake, stirring occasionally, until golden brown and crisp around the edges, 30 to 40 minutes. Remove from the oven and let cool for 5 minutes. Add the mushrooms to the large bowl with the bread.

4. Meanwhile, in a small bowl, whisk together the sherry vinegar, thyme, mustard, garlic, and the remaining 4 tablespoons olive oil. Add the tomato and stir to combine. Taste and season with salt and pepper as needed.

5. Add the tomato mixture, the Comté, and parsley to the large bowl and toss to combine. Let sit for 30 minutes before serving.

XIII

DEATH

RELEASE THE PAST TO WALK LIGHTLY INTO THE FUTURE.

Magickal Ingredient: Black sesame
Prevents unhealthy attachments

When you need to let go, Death is your friend. We all have things we need to say goodbye to: possessions, emotional patterns, ways of speaking about ourselves or others, energetic entanglements, and sometimes relationships. Death actually frees you from the pain. Just think—what if you didn't have to carry that disappointment, guilt, or prolonged grief anymore? Let's find out!

Black sesame—often used to protect negative energies from interfering with Vedic rituals—is perfect for keeping us away from anything we work to release. As a paste, black sesame brings anything it touches to the dark side with it, so put on your favorite goth jams and get into it with these Parker House rolls with black sesame butter.

PARKER HOUSE ROLLS
WITH BLACK SESAME BUTTER

SIDE —— MAKES 36 ROLLS

This take on the classic Parker House roll is a labor of love. Instead of plain melted butter, these rolls are layered with a sweet, nutty, black sesame butter. The layering gives the rolls a thin vein of black throughout that looks (and tastes) mysterious (and delicious).

You'll serve the extra butter this recipe yields with the rolls after they come out of the oven, all warm and toasty. Do not, we repeat, DO NOT brush the tops of the rolls with black sesame butter before baking, otherwise you'll have a weird, dried-up, chalky mess on your hands. (We learn things the hard way, so you don't have to.)

HOT TIP ★ IF THE BLACK SESAME BUTTER GETS TOO HARD TO SPREAD EASILY, MELT IT ON THE STOVETOP OR MICROWAVE UNTIL WARM TO THE TOUCH.

DOUGH
Butter or cooking spray, for the bowl
1½ cups whole milk, warmed to 100°F
1 (¼-ounce) envelope active dry yeast
2 tablespoons granulated sugar
4 cups all-purpose flour, plus more for dusting
1 large egg
4 tablespoons (2 ounces) unsalted butter, at room temperature
1½ teaspoons kosher salt

BLACK SESAME BUTTER
2 sticks (8 ounces) unsalted butter, melted
4 tablespoons black tahini
1 tablespoon light brown sugar
½ teaspoon kosher salt

4 tablespoons unsalted butter, melted
Flaky salt, such as Maldon

1. **MAKE THE DOUGH:** Grease a large bowl with butter or cooking spray and set aside. In the bowl of a stand mixer, combine the milk, yeast, and granulated sugar and let sit until foamy, about 10 minutes.

2. Attach the dough hook and with the mixer on medium, add the flour, egg, butter, and salt and mix until a loose dough forms. Continue mixing until the dough become smooth and elastic, about 7 minutes. Transfer the dough to the greased bowl, cover tightly with plastic wrap, and let rise in the fridge overnight.

3. Grease a 9 × 13-inch baking dish and set aside.

4. **MAKE THE BLACK SESAME BUTTER:** In a small bowl, stir together the melted butter, black tahini, brown sugar, and salt.

5. Generously dust a work surface with flour. Remove the dough from the fridge and punch it down. Turn the dough out and divide it into three equal portions. Working with one dough portion at a time, roll it into a flat rectangle roughly 6 × 16 inches. Using a pizza cutter or knife, cut the dough lengthwise into three 2-inch-wide strips and cut crosswise into four 4-inch strips for a total of 12 rectangles that measure about 2 × 4 inches.

6. Brush half of each rectangle with the black sesame butter, then fold the unbuttered half over the buttered half so the unbuttered dough hangs over the edge by about ¼ inch. (Reserve the remaining black sesame butter for serving.)

7. Place the dough in the prepared baking dish so the ¼-inch overhang overlaps the top of the folded side of the roll in front of it. Repeat with the remaining dough, until all three portions are snugly arranged 9 down and 4 across in the baking dish.

8. Brush the tops of the rolls with 2 tablespoons plain melted butter, cover with plastic wrap, and chill in the fridge for 30 minutes or up to 4 hours.

9. Preheat the oven to 350°F.

10. Bake the rolls until they have risen and the tops are golden brown, 35 to 40 minutes. Remove them from the oven and brush them liberally with the remaining 2 tablespoons of plain, melted butter. Sprinkle with flaky salt and serve with the reserved black sesame butter on the side.

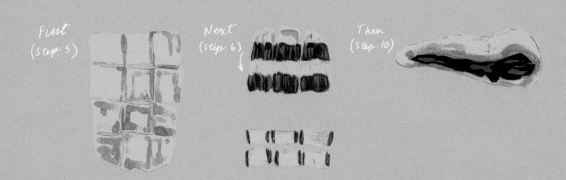

First
(step 5)

Next
(step 6)

Then
(step 10)

TEMPERANCE

XIV

AVOID EXTREMES, FIND PEACE IN MODERATION.

Magickal Ingredient: Sweet violet
Promotes emotional wellness and energetic balance

Pull in your energy, take a deep breath, and allow yourself a moment of stillness. Moderation doesn't have to be a chore. When we think of it as focusing our energy on the things that truly matter to us, it becomes a gift. Temperance affects us in a holistic way, drawing everything in so we can maintain our balance. Once we find this stillness, we get to choose how to push our energy back out again, this time in more focused ways.

To help you along, we've got a little assignment for you. With sweet violets as the centerpiece, create a party board to serve a curated gathering of people who complement each other most. And go ahead and serve booze. While the Temperance Movement shunned alcohol consumption, the Temperance archetype leaves what you moderate up to you.

ADDITIONAL MAGICKAL INGREDIENTS: HONEY, MUSTARD, OLIVES

PARTY BOARD

WITH WILDFLOWERS AND CRYSTALLIZED VIOLETS

MAIN/SNACK —— SERVES AS MANY AS YOU WANT!

There is no such thing as a bad party board, and no real way to mess this up. In fact, there isn't even really a recipe for this, just follow the steps here as a guide and make sure to have a good balance of salty and sweet options.

Use this opportunity to get to know the person behind your cheese and deli counter. Ask what they recommend. Taste some options and don't be afraid to try something new. Get weird. This truly is the most stress-free party "recipe" of all time.

Assemble your board on two actual boards (one for meats and savories and one for cheeses and sweets) or throw layers of parchment paper down directly on the table and arrange everything on that. We prefer the parchment route because you can use a marker to write the names of the charcuterie and cheeses directly on the paper.

HOT TIP ★ PLAN FOR ROUGHLY 2 TO 3 OUNCES OF MEAT AND 2 TO 3 OUNCES OF CHEESE PER PERSON.

Place three varieties of meats (including spicy and mild) on one large platter or board, and arrange three varieties of cheese (including soft and hard) on a second board. Add at least one type of snack and a spread to each board—savory additions for the meat board and fruity or nutty flavors for the cheese board. Divide the bread or crackers throughout. Don't forget to have fun.

★ **MEATS:** A spicy soppressata or chorizo; mild prosciutto, Ibérico, country ham, or finocchiona; canned fish, rillettes, or pâté (see the Giant Banh Mìs recipe on page 48)

★ **CHEESE:** Chèvre, Manchego, Brie, etc.

★ **SNACKS:** Olives, cornichons, roasted peppers, seasonal fruit, dried fruits, nuts, fresh grapes or berries

★ **SPREADS:** Honey, membrillo, jam, Nutella, grainy mustard

★ **BREADS/CRACKERS:** Water crackers, thinly sliced baguette, melba toast, or anything that piques your interest at the cracker store

★ **FLOWERS:** Garnish with wildflowers and a pile of crystallized violets (see the Magickal Ingredient Pantry on page 12) to serve.

THE DEVIL

YOU ALONE CAN LIFT THE WEIGHT OF YOUR BURDEN.

Magickal Ingredient: Rosemary
Opens and protects the heart

The Devil in the Tarot, while scary sounding, can actually come as a huge relief. It is an indicator that there is something holding us down that we have the power to break free from. So, the next time you see this card in a reading, let it be a welcome sight; know that you are ready to emerge from the heavy cloud you've been living under. This can be emotionally taxing, so it's important to keep your heart energetically cared for. Prickly, fragrant rosemary is the perfect herb for the task.

Rosemary is a popular ingredient in love spells due to its love-amplifying and protective properties. Added to salt, another powerful clearing and securing agent, it's sure to help you loosen even the most stubborn sludge.

ROSEMARY SALT(INES)

BACK POCKET BASIC (ALSO A SNACK)
MAKES ABOUT 1 CUP

Congratulations! This is the easiest recipe in the whole book because if you're dealing with Devil card energy, you already have enough on your plate (pun intended). First, you are going to make a large batch of rosemary salt, which you can then use to season anything in lieu of plain kosher salt. The salt doesn't add a huge rosemary flavor; if you blink, you'll miss it, so you really can use it on everything. People may not taste it, but you'll know it's there. The devil's in the details.

Once you get the salt made, you'll give it an official inauguration in the form of baked saltines that you can serve with the Party Board (page 159) or the Tiger Salad "Ceviche" (page 86), or eat it alone as a tasty snack.

A note from Courtney: I wanted to call this recipe "Rosemary's Baby Salt(ines)," but Melinda wouldn't let me.

⅔ cup kosher salt
⅓ cup loosely packed rosemary leaves
1 sleeve saltine crackers
1 stick (4 ounces) unsalted butter, melted
Chopped rosemary, for garnish
2 tablespoons grated parmesan cheese
   (optional)

1. Preheat the oven to 200°F. Line a sheet pan with parchment paper.

2. In a food processor (or with a mortar and pestle), combine ⅓ cup of the kosher salt and the rosemary and pulse until the rosemary has broken down, about 30 seconds. Transfer the contents to a bowl, stir in the remaining ⅓ cup salt and spread it out evenly on the prepared baking sheet.

3. Bake until it's dried out, about 30 minutes. Remove the salt, but leave the oven on and increase the temperature to 275°F.

4. Arrange the saltines on a baking sheet, then brush each one generously on both sides with the melted butter until all the butter is used. Season the top sides of each saltine with some rosemary salt, then garnish with a sprinkle of chopped rosemary. If desired, sprinkle with a little parmesan cheese.

5. Transfer to the oven and bake until lightly browned, 25 to 30 minutes.

6. Store the leftover rosemary salt in an airtight container at room temperature for up to 1 year.

XVI

THE TOWER

CRUMBLING WORLDVIEWS MAKE ROOM FOR FRESH STARTS.

Magickal Ingredient: Lavender
Calms the whole being in all situations

The Tower represents structures in our lives—ones we thought were unchangeable—crumbling before our eyes. While Tower moments are always jarring, these structures need to fall to make room for personal growth. They challenge us to find the bit of light streaming in through the cracks opening in the ground. Stay calm and follow the bread crumbs. You'll find the path to contentment.

Lavender is extremely common as a mild natural sedative, perfect for countering Tower-induced anxiety. You can find it in teas, oils, tinctures, and sachets to stash under your pillow, but we like it best in champagne. After all, that crumbling Tower is clearing the way for something better to come in. Why not throw it a welcome party?

LAVENDER CELEBRATION SPRITZ

COCKTAIL —— SERVES 14

10 lavender sprigs (about 1 ounce), plus more for serving

1¾ cups sugar

4 (750 ml) bottles (or 2 magnums) champagne or dry sparkling wine

The symbolic tower of your life just came crashing down (or maybe it hasn't yet, but it will at some point—it's inevitable). Let's celebrate! This recipe is meant for a group because it's important to be with friends and loved ones in times like these. Should we start a new paragraph here?

We like to go all out and assemble an actual champagne tower when making this because with great risk comes great reward. Yes, there is a chance your champagne tower will come crashing down, or that the champagne will go everywhere *except* in the glasses. But there is also a chance that it will work! And if it does, you will be queen of the castle. If that seems *too* risky, though, especially considering the circumstances, go ahead and make your spritzes sans tower.

1. In a saucepan, combine the lavender, sugar, and 1¾ cups water and bring to a boil over medium-high heat. Remove from the heat and let it steep at room temperature for at least 4 hours or up to overnight. Strain the syrup into a small bowl, discard the lavender, and refrigerate to chill.

2. To serve, add 1 ounce (2 tablespoons) lavender syrup to the bottom of a champagne glass and top it off with the bubbles.

Turn this tower recipe up a notch and assemble an actual tower of champagne. For this, you MUST use champagne coupe glasses. Any other type of glass will not work. And they must all be the same design of coupe glass. This isn't the time to bust out your cool vintage glass collection made up of all different styles and sizes.

1. There will be some level of spillage. Be sure to build the tower on a rimmed tray or platter to catch that spillage. And make sure the rimmed platter is on a sturdy, flat surface. The surface you build the tower on must be *completely* flat, otherwise the champagne will pour lopsidedly and only some of the glasses will be filled. So, like, get a level and be a real nerd about it.

2. Create the first layer of the tower by arranging 9 champagne coupe glasses on the tray in a square of 3 rows of 3 glasses each. Add 1 ounce (2 tablespoons) of the lavender syrup to the bottom of each glass.

3. Add 4 glasses in a 2 × 2 square on top of the 3 × 3 layer. The base of each glass on this layer should be centered directly over the diamond-shaped gaps created by the previous layer. Add 1 ounce (2 tablespoons) lavender syrup to each one of these glasses.

4. Crown the top of the tower with a single coupe glass, directly in the center, and add 1 ounce (2 tablespoons) lavender syrup to it.

5. Decorate the tray and table it's on with the extra lavender sprigs. Now gather a crowd to watch as you slowly pour champagne into the top glass. Let it fill up and overflow, trickling downward into all the glasses. Keep pouring into the top glass until they are all filled! Oh god, we really hope this works.

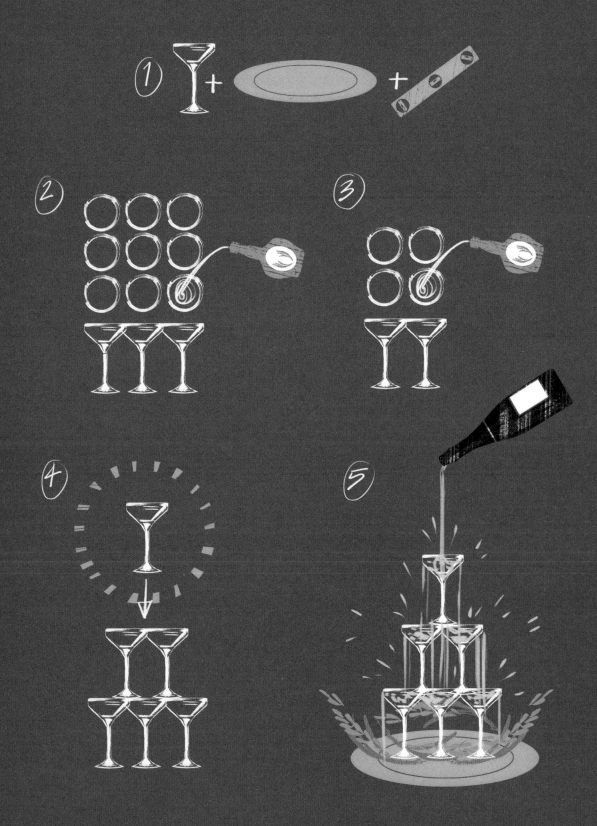

THE STAR

LET HOPE SOOTHE YOUR HEART AND LIGHT THE WAY FORWARD.

Magickal Ingredient: Honey
Provides limitless healing and faith

The earliest known written meaning of this card simply reads, "Gift." The Star urges us to remember that we are part of a great ancient lineage of creation. On the most fundamental level, we are caring and we are cared for. We are the gifts we've been waiting for, sent through time and space by our previous selves to be right here, right now. Need proof? Look back at everything you've overcome. The Star lighting the way was you.

You know what else has been around for a very, very long time? Honey. In magick and ritual, it is used to call in sweetness to the spell, for attraction, and as an offering to deities. Drink in all that gorgeous energy honey has to offer and treat yourself like a precious icon with this Gold Rush cocktail.

ADDITIONAL MAGICKAL INGREDIENT: LEMON

GOLD RUSH

COCKTAIL —— SERVES 4

The Gold Rush, invented back in the early aughts by TJ Siegal at Milk & Honey on New York City's Lower East Side, is as simple as it gets, thus proving, once again, that the sum of something is often better than its parts. We believe there is a metaphor for hope hidden somewhere in all this as well. See above re: The Star.

¼ cup honey
1 cup bourbon
4 tablespoons fresh lemon juice
Lemon peel, for garnish

1. In a medium saucepan, combine the honey and ¼ cup water and bring to a boil over medium-high heat. Remove from the heat, stir to combine, and let cool completely.

2. In a cocktail shaker, combine the bourbon, lemon juice, honey syrup, and ice and shake to chill. Fill each of four glasses with one giant ice cube and strain the Gold Rush over them. Garnish each with a piece of lemon peel.

THE MOON
DIVE DEEP WITHIN TO FACE AND CONQUER FEARS.

Magickal Ingredient: Pumpkin
Illuminates inner vision

Just as our moon reflects the light of the sun to show us its true glory, The Moon card shows us our own true reflection and urges us to be brave enough to face it. Accept the proposal by devoting time to stillness. Inward journeys require quiet contemplation in a safe place. There may be some corners that you're not ready to approach. Leave them alone. You can come back when you're ready. Go as deep as you can for as long as you can but remember to come up for air. Your inner journey will guide you in your outer life.

Give yourself some fuel for the trek. Big, bright pumpkins carry lunar energies to boost your powers of reflection and introspection. Next time you carve one for Halloween, you'll know you're not only lighting up the night, but also your receptive instincts.

PUMPKIN CORN BREAD

SIDE ── MAKES ONE 9-INCH SKILLET

This recipe is based on a classic Basque corn bread recipe, which is great news, because the Basques can really get down with corn bread. The way they do that? By adding pumpkin puree! The pumpkin doesn't add much in terms of flavor, so don't go thinking this is gonna be like the PSL of corn bread recipes. What you *will* get is a damn fine corn bread that's textured and super moist.

1 cup all-purpose flour

1 cup medium grind yellow cornmeal

1 tablespoon baking powder

1 teaspoon kosher salt

½ teaspoon baking soda

2 large eggs

1 cup buttermilk

1 cup canned unsweetened pumpkin puree

3 tablespoons unsalted butter, melted and cooled, plus 1 tablespoon butter for the skillet

1. Preheat the oven to 400°F. Place a 9-inch cast-iron skillet in the oven to warm as it preheats.

2. In a large bowl, whisk together the flour, cornmeal, baking powder, salt, and baking soda. Make a well in the center of the mixture and add the eggs, buttermilk, pumpkin puree, and 3 tablespoons melted butter. Whisk together the wet ingredients in the well (it's okay if some dry ingredients get incorporated). Using a spatula, gently combine the wet and dry ingredients until just combined.

3. Remove the skillet from the oven, add the remaining 1 tablespoon butter and swirl it around until the skillet is evenly coated. Pour the batter into the skillet and return it to the oven. Bake until it starts to brown and pull away from the edges and a toothpick inserted into the center comes out clean, 25 to 35 minutes.

4. Remove from the oven and let cool for about 10 minutes before serving.

THE SUN

BELIEVE WHAT YOUR EYES TELL YOU, FIND WHAT YOU WISH TO GROW.

Magickal Ingredient: Sunflower
Shines the light of positivity and truth

Ah, sun, glorious sun, shining down to reveal everything we need to see, lending its energy to whatever needs to grow. Stop looking for hidden meanings. Only when you truly accept what's right in front of you can you take advantage of the incredible growth potential of The Sun. And once you've got your priorities set, it's time to start intensifying that prosperous energy with sunflower power.

In addition to their obvious connection to solar energies, sunflowers are a key ingredient in many fertility spells, so they're perfect for bringing projects and ideas of any kind from conception to fruition. Crunch on this sunflower tahini salad to light up your life.

ADDITIONAL MAGICKAL INGREDIENTS: LEMON, DILL, MARJORAM, GARLIC (SEE ALLIUMS), BLACK PEPPER

SUNFLOWER TAHINI SALAD

SIDE —— SERVES 6

This is a grown-up version of Courtney's favorite childhood salad: iceberg lettuce, Hidden Valley Ranch dressing, and sunflower seeds. (She had no idea she was calling in so much positivity and truth back then!)

Speaking of ranch, is there such a thing as too much? The answer is no, which is why the ranch recipe here will make way more than you'll need. Make it a couple hours in advance and use the leftovers wisely.

SUNFLOWER TAHINI

¼ cup unsalted roasted sunflower seeds
2 tablespoons fresh lemon juice
3 tablespoons extra-virgin olive oil
¼ teaspoon kosher salt

SALAD

1 head iceberg lettuce, roughly chopped or torn (about 8 cups)
1 cup shredded carrots
1 cup roughly chopped (mini) cucumbers
¼ cup ranch dressing, store-bought or homemade (recipe follows)
Kosher salt and freshly ground black pepper
Sunflower seeds, for garnish

1. MAKE THE SUNFLOWER TAHINI: In a food processor or blender, combine the sunflower seeds, 2½ tablespoons water, the lemon juice,

olive oil, and salt and process on high for about 30 seconds, or until a smooth paste forms. Scrape the mixture into a small bowl.

2. ASSEMBLE THE SALAD: In a large bowl, toss together the iceberg, carrots, cucumber, and ranch dressing. Taste and add salt and pepper as needed.

3. Drizzle the sunflower tahini on top, garnish with sunflower seeds, and serve immediately.

MEANWHILE, BACK AT THE . . . RANCH

MAKES ABOUT 2 CUPS

½ cup mayonnaise
½ cup sour cream
½ cup buttermilk
1 tablespoon distilled white vinegar
1 tablespoon Louisiana-style hot sauce
2 tablespoons chopped fresh dill
1 tablespoon chopped fresh marjoram or oregano
2 teaspoons chopped fresh chives
1 teaspoon garlic powder
Kosher salt and freshly ground black pepper

In a medium bowl, whisk together the mayonnaise, sour cream, buttermilk, vinegar, hot sauce (if using), dill, marjoram, chives, and garlic powder. Taste and add salt and pepper as needed. Cover the dressing and let refrigerate for at least 2 hours. Store in an airtight container in the fridge for up to 1 week.

XX

JUDGMENT

EXCAVATION OF THE PAST BRINGS CLOSURE AND A HEALTHIER TOMORROW.

Magickal Ingredient: Flaxseed
Brings old wounds forward to heal

Judgment as a concept tends to feel negative, but it is necessary for sound decision-making and psychic housekeeping. Like Marie Kondo tells us to do with clothes and books, pull all those old memories and lessons from your past and subconscious so you can sort them out. Keep what is helping you make good decisions in the present, toss out what is better left behind (thank it first!). When digging up the past, we are bound to reopen a few wounds along the way. Flaxseed is here to soothe.

Flaxseed is protective as well as healing, so you get a nice little zone to do your work in. You can sprinkle them on yogurt or toss them in a smoothie, but we personally think they are best served in these muffins.

ADDITIONAL MAGICKAL INGREDIENTS: BANANA, VANILLA

BANANA FLAXSEED MUFFINS

SNACK —— MAKES 12 MUFFINS

This book was written in the spring of 2020. It was a wild time. People baked a *ton* of banana bread. This recipe is an ode to that.

Use this muffin base as a springboard for whatever extras your heart desires. Add mini chocolate chips, berries, shredded coconut, toasted nuts, or nothing at all! Just make sure the bananas are super-duper ripe.

1½ **cups all-purpose flour**

¼ **cup flaxseed meal**

¾ **cup sugar**

1 **teaspoon baking soda**

1 **teaspoon baking powder**

½ **teaspoon kosher salt**

1½ **cups mashed bananas (from about 3 large bananas)**

¾ **cup whole milk**

1 **large egg**

5 **tablespoons unsalted butter, melted**

1 **teaspoon pure vanilla extract**

½ **cup chopped walnuts or semisweet chocolate chips (optional)**

1. Preheat the oven to 425°F. Grease 12 cups of a muffin tin or line with paper liners.

2. In a large bowl, whisk together the flour, flaxseed meal, sugar, baking soda, baking powder, and salt. Make a well in the center of the mixture and add the mashed banana, milk, egg, melted butter, and vanilla. Whisk together the wet ingredients in the well (it's okay if some dry ingredients get incorporated). Using a spatula, combine the wet and dry ingredients until fully incorporated. Fold in any additional mix-ins (if using).

3. Divide the batter evenly among the muffin cups, filling each three-quarters of the way. Bake until a toothpick inserted into the center of a muffin comes out clean, 22 to 25 minutes. Store any leftover muffins at room temperature in an airtight container for up to 4 days.

THE WORLD

ONE WORLD ENDS AND ANOTHER BEGINS.
STEP INTO THE PORTAL.

Magickal Ingredient: Dandelion
Cleanses the physical and energetic body

We often talk about transitions in life as moving from one chapter to another, but that's not quite right. There is a space in between where we lose our bearings a little, our vision goes blurry, and a sense of uncertainty creeps in. That's the moment we decide to get scared or get psyched. We recommend the latter. Stepping into a new world allows us to reflect on what we've left behind and determine what lessons to take with us. As we step through, it is good practice to do some magickal cleansing, and dandelion really does the trick.

All parts of the plant can be used for cleansing of the physical and nonphysical bodies. Dandelion tea has been used as a liver tonic since at least the 1600s. In magick, it is said to clear negative energies and open perception. Shift your perception of this common weed with our wilted dandelion greens.

ADDITIONAL MAGICKAL INGREDIENT: BLACK PEPPER

WILTED DANDELION GREENS
WITH APPLES AND PANCETTA

SIDE —— SERVES 4

Dandelion greens are in season in the late winter and throughout spring. They are really bitter (like, *really* bitter), but never fear, the sweetness of the apples and the fat from the pancetta round out this simple dish perfectly.

To the uninitiated, pancetta is basically unsmoked bacon. You can usually find it already cubed in the cured meat section of the grocery store. Fancy butcher shops will also sell it, but you'll probably have to cube it yourself. In a pinch, you can always use bacon.

HOT TIP ★ IF YOU HAVE PROBLEMS SOURCING DANDELION GREENS, THIS RECIPE ALSO WORKS WITH CHARD, KALE, OR MUSTARD GREENS. YOU'LL NEED ABOUT 15 CUPS OF LOOSELY PACKED GREENS TO MAKE THIS. (WE KNOW IT SOUNDS LIKE A LOT, BUT IT COOKS DOWN, WAY DOWN.)

4 bunches dandelion greens (about 1 pound), stems removed
3 ounces pancetta, cut into ½-inch cubes
1 Granny Smith apple, cored and cut into ½-inch dice
3 tablespoons apple cider vinegar
Kosher salt and freshly ground black pepper

1. Slice or tear the greens into roughly 2-inch-wide strips. In a large skillet, brown the pancetta over medium heat until crispy, about 7 minutes. Remove the pancetta from the heat and transfer to a small bowl lined with paper towels.

2. Pour out all but 1 tablespoon of fat from the skillet. Add the apple and sauté over high heat until lightly browned, about 3 minutes. Transfer the apples to the same large bowl.

3. Reduce the heat to medium-high and add the dandelion greens in batches, letting the previous batch wilt before adding more greens. Once all the greens are in the skillet, season with salt, add ¼ cup water, and continue cooking until evaporated and the greens are wilted and soft, 3 to 4 minutes. Transfer the greens to the large bowl, add the vinegar, and toss to coat. Taste and add salt and pepper as needed.

4. Serve immediately.

SPELLS

Ready to really earn your broomstick? You'll need to cast a spell. Putting a variety of magickal things together to influence a specific sphere of energy is the basic nature of a spell. We got you started by putting together some menus from this book that work well together both magickly and as a meal.

Once you get the hang of it, you can explore different combinations of recipes and ingredients to suit your needs. Manipulate the recipes as needed and feel free to round any of these menus out with side dishes, salads, or wine to make them complete.

ABUNDANCE

A Rose Is a Rose Is a Rosé Punch
(EMPRESS) 141

Tiger Salad "Ceviche"
(THREE OF CUPS) 86

Loaded Baked Potato Pot Stickers
(THREE OF COINS) 110

Veggie Muffuletta
(TEN OF COINS) 122

ADD TO THE ATMOSPHERE: JEWEL TONE LINENS ★ GREEN CANDLES
BIG BOUQUETS ★ PYRITE ★ EMERALD ★ PERIDOT

CELEBRATION

Butterfly Pea Flower Cinnamon Gimlet
(THE MAGICIAN) 137

Grilled Oysters with Chili-Lime Butter
(NINE OF CUPS) 96

Yucatan-Style Lamb Shoulder Tacos
(SIX OF WANDS) 67

ADD TO THE ATMOSPHERE: PATTERNED LINENS ★ A RAINBOW OF CANDLES
STREAMERS ★ PARTY HATS ★ CONFETTI ★ CHRYSANTHEMUMS
PEACOCK ORE ★ LEMON QUARTZ

CLARITY

Slayer of Pain
(WHEEL OF FORTUNE) 150

BBQ Chicken French Bread Pizzas
(SEVEN OF SWORDS) 42

Ancho Chile Brownies
(KING OF WANDS) 81

ADD TO THE ATMOSPHERE: LIGHT- AND DARK-BLUE LINENS ★ LIGHT-BLUE CANDLES
PINE BOUGHS ★ LAPIS LAZULI ★ AQUAMARINE

CREATIVITY

**Classic Michelada
with Tajín-Cayenne Salt**

**A Big Ol' Cauldron of
Ranch-Style Beans**

Sunflower Tahini Salad

**Crispy Ground Beef
and Pickle Tacos**

ADD TO THE ATMOSPHERE: ORANGE LINENS AND CANDLES ★ DAISIES
SUNFLOWERS ★ ORANGE CALCITE ★ RUBY

EMPOWERMENT

Moscow Mule Melon Slushies

(STRENGTH) 148

Giant Roast Pork Sandwiches

(TEN OF WANDS) 72

Baked Alaska with Cinnamon Toast Crumbs

(KNIGHT OF SWORDS) 52

ADD TO THE ATMOSPHERE: WARM TONE LINENS AND CANDLES
GINGER BLOSSOMS ★ CITRINE ★ CARNELIAN

FRESH START

**Crudo with Grapefruit
and Avocado**
(SEVEN OF CUPS) 92

**Wilted Dandelion Greens
with Apples and Pancetta**
(THE WORLD) 172

**Bone-In Cowperson Steak
with Sesame Chili Oil**
(TWO OF WANDS) 59

**Make-Ahead Chocolate Soufflé
with Amaro Sauce**
(QUEEN OF SWORDS) 54

ADD TO THE ATMOSPHERE: BRIGHTLY COLORED LINENS ★ WHITE CANDLES
CAMELLIAS ★ TULIPS ★ MOSS AGATE ★ AMETHYST

LETTING GO

ADD TO THE ATMOSPHERE: BLACK AND WHITE LINENS ★ BLACK CANDLES
DAHLIAS ★ BLACK TOURMALINE ★ GREEN CALCITE

PEACE

ADD TO THE ATMOSPHERE: LINENS IN SOFT COLORS ★ WHITE CANDLES
LAVENDER ★ LILAC ★ QUARTZ CRYSTAL ★ LEPIDOLITE

ROMANTIC LOVE

Pomegranate Julep
(THE HIGH PRIESTESS) 138

Pickled Veggies
(FOUR OF COINS) 113

**Pan-Fried Cod
with Spicy Rémoulade**
(TWO OF CUPS) 85

**Vanilla Panna Cotta
with Sherry Gastrique**
(THE LOVERS) 144

ADD TO THE ATMOSPHERE: GREEN AND/OR PINK LINENS AND CANDLES
ROSES ★ ROSE QUARTZ ★ AVENTURINE

ACKNOWLEDGMENTS

To the Clarkson Potter fam—Sara Neville, Ian Dingman, Gabrielle Van Tassel, Serena Wang, Heather Williamson, Chloe Aryeh, and Felix Cruz. Your insight and prowess made this book even better than we thought possible. You are all a pleasure to work with and we thank you from the bottom of our very full hearts (and stomachs). Thank you for seeing the magick in our bag of dinner party tricks.

We are over the moon (literally! We flew up on our broomsticks) to have such incredible artists bring this vision to life. Kim Thompson, it's time to confess—we have a MASSIVE crush on your illustrations. We hope this doesn't make things weird. Kristin Teig, Nidia Cueva, Caroline Hwang—you are the absolute photo shoot dream team! We'll always have that one windy day in November . . .

A million thanks to Chelsey Bawot and Codii Lopez for braving pandemic-era grocery stores to recipe test this cookbook. We would have gone off the deep end for sure without your talent and expertise. Three of Cups in the house!

Kumi Nazel, you've been with me (Courtney) since the Large Marge days. Thank you for all your help throughout the years and your help with the cocktail creations in this book. You are an amazing human.

Eve Atterman. What a ride! This book would not exist without you. May our Mercury retrograde-power-coven continue to defy convention and make dreams come true.

FROM COURTNEY:
To my family and chosen family in Texas, New York, Los Angeles, and everywhere in between. If I named each of you, it would take up too many pages, but you know who you are. (If you aren't sure, shoot me a text and I'll confirm.) I love you all so much. To all the members of the Hot Dog Appreciation Club. It's people like you who give me hope in this crazy, mixed-up world. Melinda Lee Holm, thank you for putting up with me throughout the process of making of this book. You didn't give me Rosemary's Baby Salt, but you've given me a soundboard, the grounding energy that I desperately need ALL of the time (I'm sure you've noticed) and so much more, I can't fit it all here. You are my BFF for life and I love you always. Next stop: PJs on PJs!

FROM MELINDA:
Anne Woodward, my manager and friend, I don't know what I'd do or where I'd be without you and I hope I never have to find out. Thank you for keeping my sanity intact and my laughter flowing. Chris, my love, you were definitely head cheerleader in another life. Your unwavering enthusiasm for and support of everything I do is the stuff of dreams. I am so lucky to have you.

And my dear Courtney McBroom, my co-conspirator, my sister from another mister (and mistress), thank you for knowing what we were sitting on with all these magickal food experiments, for being a brilliant and hilarious chef, and most of all for being so damn easy to love. We did it again!

INDEX

Published in the United States by Clarkson
Potter/Publishers, an imprint of Random House,
a division of Penguin Random House LLC,
New York.
clarksonpotter.com

CLARKSON POTTER is a trademark and
POTTER with colophon is a registered trademark
of Penguin Random House LLC.

Library of Congress Cataloging-in-Publication
Data is available upon request.

ISBN 978-0-593-23214-9
eBook ISBN 978-0-593-23215-6

Printed in China

Editor: Sara Neville
Designer: Ian Dingman
Production Editor: Serena Wang
Production Manager: Heather Williamson
Copy Editor: Kate Slate
Indexer: Jay Kreider

10 9 8 7 6 5 4 3 2 1

First Edition

**Bone-in
Cowperson Steak**
(Two of Wands)

Slayer of Pain
(Wheel of Fortune)

**Grilled Oysters
with Chili
Lime Butter**
(Nine of Cups)

**BBQ Chicken French
Bread Pizzas**
(Seven of Swords)